Person-Centred Counselling

An Experiential Approach

David L. Rennie

ISBN 0-7619-5344-2 (hbk)   ISBN-13 978-0-7619-5344-9 (hbk)
ISBN 0-7619-5345-0 (pbk)   ISBN-13 978-0-7619-5345-6 (pbk)

© David L. Rennie, 1998
First published 1998
Reprinted 2002, 2004, 2006, 2007

Apart from any fair dealing for the purposes of research or private study, or criticism or review, as permitted under the Copyright, Designs and Patents Act, 1988, this publication may be reproduced, stored or transmitted in any form or by any means, only with the prior permission in writing of the publishers, or in the case of reprographic reproduction, in accordance with the terms of licences issued by the Copyright Licensing Agency. Inquiries concerning reproduction outside those terms should be sent to the publishers.

SAGE Publications Ltd
1 Oliver's Yard, 55 City Road
London EC1Y 1SP

SAGE Publications Inc
2455 Teller Road
Thousand Oaks, California 91320

SAGE Publications India Pvt Ltd
B 1/11 Mohan Cooperative Industrial Area
Mathura Road.
New Delhi 110 044
India

SAGE Publications Asia-Pacific Pte Ltd
33 Pekin Street #02-01
Far East Square
Singapore 048763

British Library Cataloguing in Publication data

A catalogue record for this book is available
from the British Library

Library of Congress catalog card number 97062420

Typeset by Photoprint Ltd., Torquay, Devon
Printed digitally and bound in Great Britain by
Biddles Ltd., King's Lynn, Norfolk

Contents

Preface   iv

1 Situating the Approach   1

2 The Client as Agent   13

3 The First Meeting   22

4 Basic Attending Skills   32

5 Vivid Language: Liberating the Secondary Stream of Consciousness   44

6 Transparency in the Relationship with the Client   60

7 Process Identification and Process Direction   71

8 Metacommunication   89

9 Tying it All Together: the Working Alliance   102

10 Training   126

11 Conclusion   143

References   144

Subject index   151

Author index   154

Preface

Carl Rogers is widely hailed for his humanism and, of course, for the approach to counselling that often bears his name. Yet he was a deeply divided individual. As an American he was swept up in American pragmatism and, despite his deep respect for the individual and for the subjectivity of human experience, he failed to appreciate fully the nature and significance of consciousness. As a therapist, he was shy and, although unsurpassed in his ability to be empathic and supportive, never adequately dealt with the interpersonal relationship between counsellor and client. As a producer of knowledge, he operated hermeneutically as a theorist but positivistically as a scientist.

Following in Rogers's wake, person-centred and experiential counsellors and therapists have similarly taken on the best and the worst of modernism. They have embraced humanistic individualism and, with it, subjectivity. This ontology has allowed them to value human dignity in ways not seen in psychoanalysis, behavioural therapy and even cognitive therapy. They have also subscribed to objectivism and the correspondence theory of truth, however, which has prevented them from embracing fully the qualities of human 'beingness' that their ontology entails. Meanwhile, postmodernists have been been snapping at their heels, challenging that experiencing is shot through with social constructionism.

The current approach to counselling was developed with one foot – but only one – in the person-centred and experiential mainstream. I have been privileged to be a member of a university department that has been home to Laura Rice and Les Greenberg, both leaders in person-centred and experiential counselling/therapy, while not being involved in their research programmes. After a stint of using natural science methods in my early years in the department, I changed to qualitative methodology. Over the years since that decision, the adoption of the alternative method has led me to enquire into basic questions of the nature of the person and whether or not it is possible for people to develop knowledge objectively.

All of these considerations were stimulated by my enquiry into the client's subjective experience of counselling and were brought to bear on that same enquiry. Freed from positivism, I have gradually come to realize that qualitative research – at least the way my research group has been practising it – is, at root, hermeneutical. Thus, we are now doing the same kind of work that Rogers did as a theorist. Rather than seeing such work as a means to the end of experimental confirmation, however, we consider it to be good science in its own right. The enquiry has involved asking people about their experience and interpreting what they say while staying close to their language. The method has allowed us to be radically empirical, to attempt to understand the meaning of verbal reports on experience.

Much of what has informed the current approach to counselling represented in this book has to do with what clients have told me about what counselling is like for them. Their reports have made me realize how keenly interested they are in what counsellors think of them and in how counsellors deal with them. It has also made me aware, with great force, of the extent to which clients are active – discursively and silently – in managing their relationship both with themselves and with their counsellor.

The approach thus revolves around clients' and counsellors' reflexivity, defined as self-awareness and the agency involved in and flowing from it. This concept opens the door to the significance of matters such as silent experiencing, the balance of power between the client and counsellor, and the importance of their communication about their communication. The implications of reflexivity are thus far-reaching, extending into all levels of practice and all forms of person-centred and experiential counselling. Moreover, the approach represented in the book has strong affiliations with feminist therapy, existential therapy and interpersonal therapy, and has implications for them as well. In this sense, it is my hope that the book will have integrative impact – something that is sorely needed given the contemporary threat to humanistic counselling approaches imposed by their putatively more empirically oriented and efficient brethren. The approach represented here has an eye on efficiency while adhering fervently to humanism.

This book began as a training manual that I wrote ten years ago. Over the years of its use, a number of students have commented on it, for which I am grateful. More recently, John McLeod encouraged me to expand it and submit it for publication. Once in the capable hands of Susan Worsey of Sage, the manual was turned over to Dave Mearns and Brian Thorne to add to John's review, and both were convinced that the approach represented in it falls somewhere within the person-centred tradition, although I would have to position it. After further consideration of the literature, I decided that it fits between the person-centred and experiential genres, hence the title.

In recognition of the approach having been influenced by the reports of clients in counselling, I owe a huge debt to those who participated in my research and their counsellors who encouraged the participation, some of whom participated themselves. My students Pavla Reznicek, Yaacov Lefcoe and Kimberley Watson were able research assistants throughout the project and I am grateful for their contributions. As always, my wife Judy has been wonderful in her support.

David Rennie

1
Situating the Approach

The counselling described in this book is in keeping with those that share Carl Rogers's deep interest in working within the client's frame of reference but do not subscribe strictly to Rogerian theory and practice. It thus joins the broad category of person-centred and experiential counselling and psychotherapy approaches described by Lietaer as:

> the classic Rogerians; the client-centered therapists who are in favour of some form of integration or even eclecticism; the Gendlians, for whom the whole focusing approach is a precious way of working; the client-centered therapists who look at the therapy process in information-processing terms; the client-centered therapists for whom the interpersonal aspect, the here-and-now of interaction between the client and therapist is their central focus, and maybe some other suborientations or combinations of them. (1989, p. 17)

Like the orthodox or, as Shlien (1970) terms it, the 'literal' person-centred approach, the present one places its main emphasis on the client's experience, choice and personal freedom and makes following the client's lead a priority. It both differs from the literal approach in some respects and adds to it. Rather than traditional Rogerian theory, it is organized around the concept of reflexivity, which I have defined as self-awareness and agency within that self-awareness (Rennie, 1992, 1997).[1] Moreover, as much emphasis is placed on the counsellor's reflexivity as on the client's, which brings the counsellor's process into the picture equally with the client's. A high value is placed on the counsellor's demystification of his or her presence in the counselling transaction through the activity of being open about what he or she is up to, so long as doing so does not detract from the focus on the client. In this regard, it contributes to the emphasis being placed in many quarters on counsellor transparency. The approach also draws upon metacommunication as practised in most forms of interpersonal therapy, while going beyond the conceptualization and application of metacommunication as used in that form of therapy. Finally, the approach entails counsellor directiveness of the client's processing of experience when it seems warranted by both client and counsellor.

It is the counsellor's guidance of the client's processing of experience that gives rise to the book's subtitle: *An Experiential Approach*. Yet, as will be seen, the process work outlined is non-technical. It takes the form either of directing clients' attention to the cognitive activity in which they appear to be currently engaged or of suggesting that they might engage in a particular process. This kind of process work is integral to the flow of the client's experience and fits smoothly into the emphasis on empathic responding characteristic of the literal approach. At the same time, it constitutes a bridge between that mode of responding and the more technical experiential approaches, if the counsellor is so inclined.

In terms of Lietaer's classification, then, the implicit assumptions and practices involved in the approach position it between the literal person-centred approach and therapies characterized by, as Rice (1974) succinctly put it, the therapist being directive in terms of the client's process and non-directive regarding content. These therapies include Gendlin's experiential therapy (Gendlin, 1981, 1996), the process-experiential approach developed by Rice and Greenberg (Greenberg, 1984; Greenberg, Rice and Elliott, 1993; Rice and Saperia, 1984) and the perceptual-processing approach advanced by Toukmanian (1986, 1990, 1992). There are, of course, many differences that separate these various 'directive' approaches. Gendlin's is holistic whereas the process-experiential and perceptual-processing approaches draw upon information-processing theory and are more reductionistic. In this respect, the current approach is more in keeping with Gendlin's holism. The middle ground occupied by the approach is thus compatible with the views of thinkers and practitioners such as Mearns (1994; Mearns and Thorne, 1988), Thorne (1989; Mearns and Thorne, 1988), Lietaer (1984), Sachse (1989), Liejssen (1990),[2] Holdstock (1996) and O'Hara (1984), among others.

In the remainder of this introductory chapter, I consider these points more fully. I begin with the quality of reflexivity. Following that, I address how this approach and the theory supporting it compare with the others in terms of self-actualization, the necessity and sufficiency of the core conditions, experience and its leading edge, and holism.

Reflexivity and its embodiment

The most significant quality of 'human beingness' is our ability to think about ourselves, to think about our thinking, to feel about our feelings, to treat ourselves as objects of our attention and to use what we find there as a point of departure in deciding what to do next. This is reflexivity as I understand it. Many thinkers attach significance to reflexivity in terms of its implications for the concept of self but its importance is much broader; reflexivity is a major feature of consciousness and is integral to action. I was led to its pervasiveness after interviewing clients about their moment-to-moment experience of counselling/therapy (e.g. Rennie, 1984, 1990, 1992, 1994a, 1996). By virtue of reflexivity we can intervene into ourselves, make decisions, change ourselves. This is not to say that this capacity is total. The evidence for unconscious determination of actions, for societal constraints on change and for resistance to change is indisputable. But these considerations should not be allowed to diminish the centrality of reflexivity in our experience. We move in and out of streams of thought, just as we move into and out of various bodily activities associated with them. At one moment, we are 'in' a stream of thought; we are not aware that we are – we just 'are' (see Searle, 1983). The next moment or hour, as the case may be, the stream ceases, enabling us to be aware that we were in the stream. In that moment of awareness, we may either undeliberatively think of something else and go along with that thought, or deliberate on what to attend to next and enter the stream resulting from that decision, thus the repeating cycle. This is consciousness – an ongoing alternation of non-reflexive and reflexive thought.

Thinking is activity. We know this because when someone asks us what we are doing when we are immersed in thought, it is perfectly natural and correct to reply, 'I'm thinking'. For this and other reasons given in Chapter 2, I make no attempt to separate reflexivity and agency. They are part of each other in that agency is purposive activity emanating from reflexive activity and returning to it (Rennie, 1997).

There are reasons for being suspicious of reflexivity, especially if one is a client or a counsellor helping a client. In the act of attending to ourselves, we can detach from ourselves, as when we distance ourselves from painful feelings while allowing ourselves to be aware of what the feelings are about. Still we may not distance thought from our experience in this way. It is possible to draw our attention to our feelings as well as to our thoughts. Furthermore, although we are not capable of thinking about what we are thinking in precisely the same instant, we are capable of being aware of what we are feeling in a given instant. The reason the first is true is that we cannot think and be aware of that thinking simultaneously. Instead, either we think without being aware of it, or we think about what we just thought or should next think about; we cannot catch in action the 'I' that instigates activity. Interestingly the same does not seem to be true of feeling, at least not to the same extent. Somehow, feeling is 'there' – an ongoing presence – ready for scanning and symbolization. Feeling seems to be in a different place than our thoughts; it seems to be in our bodies.

Some philosophers are sceptical of reflexivity precisely because of its implicit dualism. This was true of Dewey who, in his attempt to overcome philosophical problems raised by dualism, combined Darwinism with the Romantic idea of growth and created a form of monistic naturalism in which human functioning (including thinking) is action in the service of adaptation and growth (Rennie, 1998). Dewey had a tacit but strong influence on Rogers (Van Belle, 1980) and the vestiges of this influence can be seen in many of his followers as well. Rogers and the literalists (e.g. Bozarth, 1984, 1990a; Bozarth and Brodley, 1986; Patterson, 1990; Shlien, 1996) appear to mistrust reflexivity, instead placing more trust in a non-reflexive union of feeling and action. This is not to say that they have discounted reflexivity totally. Influenced by Gendlin, particularly, Rogers realized increasingly that we have a felt-sense to which we can attend and that doing so is an important step towards the productive processing of experience. For Rogers, however, full functioning is non-reflexive: a union of feeling and thought and behaviour. Thus, Rogers never put much stock in the concept of the ego (Van Belle, 1980). Instead, very much like Dewey, his ontology is closer to a monistic processing of experience.[3]

Gendlin's experiential approach to therapy, on the other hand, engages reflexivity. Gendlin maintains that embodied meaning as a felt-sense is a *direct referent* (e.g. Gendlin, 1962) or, more recently, an *exact form* (Gendlin, 1990) available for symbolization (the claim that it is thus analogous to a Husserlian 'essence' is debatable; cf. Gendlin, 1978/1979, 1990; Sass, 1988; see also Greenberg, Rice and Elliott, 1993). Thus, we can and should direct our attention to our felt-sense. This is a prescription of active reflexivity and is explicitly dualistic, for which Gendlin has been unfairly criticized (Leijssen, 1990; Wexler, 1974). There is a difference between subject–object and mind–body dualism (with the latter being exemplified by Descartes's characterization of mind and body as separate substances). As Gendlin is well aware, contemporary philosophical thought is moving in the direction of characterizing human beingness as non-reductive, *incarnated* embodiment and thus disputes substance dualism (e.g. Merleau-

Ponty, 1962; for an Anglo-American perspective, see Margolis, 1986, 1987). Reflexivity is but another aspect of that same incarnated embodiment, in that people have the ability to look at themselves as 'objects'. Hence, there is nothing special about reflexivity. It is simply the most wonderful quality of being human (Donald, 1991; May, 1958a).[4,5]

In contrast, the process-experiential and perceptual-processing therapists are midway between the literal Rogerians and the Gendlians in terms of the recognition and application of reflexivity. For example, especially in their recent work that emphasizes the importance of emotion in therapeutic change (e.g. Greenberg, Rice and Elliott, 1993), the process-experiential therapists employ the Gendlian focusing technique when clients have difficulty making contact with their emotions. Thus, focusing is used as a means to the end of contacting (hypothesized) emotion schemes so that a given task (such as resolving a conflict split, dealing with unfinished business, resolving a problematic reaction to a past event, and so on) can proceed.

Reflexivity and silent activity

In the reflexive moment we are in a position to choose what to do next, and how. When engaged in discourse, in what seems like a rapid series of feedback loops, we sense the possible impact – on the other person and on ourselves – of expressing a thought or feeling. We are guided by this sense in deciding whether or not to express an inner experience at all, and, if proceeding, in managing how much of it we express and how we go about expressing it. This monitoring is done feelingly and seemingly almost instantaneously but is reflexive all the same.

In the counselling situation, such self-monitoring goes on in clients as much as in counsellors, of course. The result is a complex and dynamic situation in which the conscious goings-on between the counsellor and client variously occur on either one or two levels, depending on whether each person is conversing non-reflexively or reflexively. Non-reflexive talk is simply the talk itself, within which those involved in discussion are not deliberating on what they are saying but rather are just saying it in expression of an intention in the process of fulfilment. Reflexive talk, on the other hand, involves thoughts and feelings *between* utterances in the way described.

Accordingly, in the present approach, great significance is attached to silent activity. Rogers and his literalist followers appear to recognize such activity implicitly but, seemingly because of their tacitly monistic ontology, do not accord it the attention it deserves. In the same vein, with the exception of the work by J.C. Watson (e.g. Watson, 1997; Watson and Greenberg, 1994; Watson and Rennie, 1994), the members of the process-experiential group do not make much of such covert, conscious control because of their interest in stimulating the client's activation and *expression* of non-reflexive cognitive/affective schemes. Toukmanian addresses tacitly the significance of covert experience through her valuing of controlled as compared with automatic perceptual processing, with the former having to do with reflexivity. In contrast, Gendlin recognizes covert experience explicitly when he encourages clients to work silently when focusing. Gendlin pays comparatively less attention to the client's silent experience of the therapist and of the therapy relationship, however. The approach put forward by Mearns (1994) is closest to the present one in recognizing and attempting to work productively with the full implications of silent activity.

Self-actualization and the necessity and sufficiency of the core conditions

Rogers and the literalists hold that all organisms have an actualizing tendency. The emphasis is on growth, optimal conditions for it, and individualism. As part of his most thorough theoretical statement, Rogers wrote:

> It should be noted that this basic actualizing tendency is the only motive which is postulated in this theoretical system. It should also be noted that it is the organism as a whole, and only the organism as a whole, which exhibits this tendency. There are no homunculi, no other sources of energy or action in the system. The self, for example, is an important construct in our theory, but the self does not 'do' anything. It is only one expression of the general tendency of the organism to behave in those ways which maintain and enhance the self.[6] (1959, p. 196)

In this same work, Rogers (1959) distinguishes between actualization of the organism and actualization of the self. Self-actualization may or may not be congruent with actualization of the organism, depending on the compatibility of organismic and societal influences on self-development. Thus, some social conditions are more conducive to growth than others. In the interests of adaptation and in response to conditional regard, individuals comply and identify with social admonitions in order to reduce conflict with the social environment. This reduction in conflict is achieved at the expense of inducing conflict with organismic experiencing, however. The result is incongruence (see Ford, 1991). In order to achieve congruence, it is necessary for individuals to encounter the antidote to conditional regard so that they can safely contact and identify with their suppressed organismic promptings. In his famous statement, Rogers (1957) proposes that six conditions, highlighted by the therapist's three attitudes of empathy, unconditional positive regard and congruence, are both necessary and sufficient as conditions for positive therapeutic change in that they determine the client's establishment of congruence with organismic experiencing.

Rogers's and the literalists' belief in self-actualization as defined appears to be the source of their respect for the uniqueness of the individual. It is also the origin of their belief that individuals can change themselves given the right conditions. Moreover, inherent in the concept of self-actualization is the belief that the growth impetus is intrinsically towards goodness. Hence, this theory is profoundly Romantic and even mystical, much as Dewey's belief in growth is seen by some as mystical (Murphy, 1951; Thayer, 1968).

I have further difficulty with the theory of self-actualization because it fails to account for a great deal of what we know about people, particularly in terms of their negative aspects. As Land (1996) remarks, it is not easy to reconcile the concept of inherent, organismic goodness with the existence of so much evil in the world. For Land, support for the notion of organismic actualization comes from faith more than evidence (see also O'Hara, 1995; Wood, 1996).

Alternatives to the concept of organismic evaluation and self-actualization have been proposed by experientially inclined therapists as well as by existential ones. Gendlin (1974) suggests that the felt-sense should be substituted for the organismic valuing process. This suggestion is an improvement in that it addresses experience that is immediate and is not burdened with the mysticism surrounding organismic evaluation. Butler and Rice (1963) propose that there are three main classes of drives (maintenance, emergency and pain, and developmental) and two levels of activation (chronic and acute). This formulation encompasses the complexity of motivation more fully than does the singular concept of organismic actualization and, correspondingly, allows for the possibility that some people actively resist change and so change very slowly, if at all. Similarly, conceptualizing within the existential perspective, Maddi (1988) suggests that growth entails possibility but may be precluded by facticity, or facts having to do with 'human beingness' (Heidegger coined this term to denote that facts having to do with *Dasein* (being – here/there) are different than facts having to do with things). In a tacit criticism of self-actualization, Maddi proposes the alternative concept of *hardiness*, meaning that some people are hardy and hence open to change whereas others are less so. Therapy for unhardy people goes through three stages: the exploration of facticity and possibility, hopefully leading to the successful taking of challenges; if that fails, the instigation of focusing to get into the repressed emotion; and if that fails, the coming to terms with no change. Other criticisms of Rogers's self-actualization theory have been made (e.g. Seeman, 1988; Wexler, 1974).

The literalists' claim to person-centred therapy seems unduly exclusionary to practitioners and theorists who (a) deeply believe in the relationship more as person-to-person than agent-to-patient; (b) like nothing better than following the client's lead; yet (c) recognize that for some clients the prospect of changing is more disturbing than the prospect of staying the same, regardless of whatever impulse they may have to change; and (d) are sceptical about the claim that the Rogerian core conditions determine positive personality change (Rogers, 1957). The position taken in this book is that the core conditions are necessary and *perhaps* sufficient. Apart from the empirical evidence indicating that the conditions are not always sufficient, especially for clients who do not process their experience well (e.g. Rogers, 1961), the tenability of this proposition is called into question if we grant that people may be patients as well as agents. Under the assumption that the client is motivated to change for the better (an assumption that does not require the notion of self-actualization), Rogers's if-then proposition is tenable if it may be assumed that the client is primarily an agent as opposed to a patient. However, if the person is effectively controlled by aspects of his or her beingness, whether in the form of extreme feelings or unconscious structures and processes of various sorts, then he or she is a patient, by virtue of that control (Macmurray, 1957).

The question then arises as to whether or not people who are primarily agential, but nevertheless insufficiently agential to be able to solve their problems on their own, may solve them in the presence of an empathic, positively regarding and congruent therapist. The position taken in this book is that the answer to this question is a definite 'Yes'. Alternatively, clients may be patients more than agents in relation to their troubles, in which case, given assent, the counsellor may have to seize the reins for a while until the client can take over. It is unlikely that the client's cooperation could be gained in the absence of the core conditions which means that they are necessary but not sufficient in such a case.

In this respect, then, the approach outlined in this book is in the 'directive' camp in its recognition that, depending on the circumstances, the therapist may expedite the progress of therapy by being directive about the client's processing of experience. A feature of the approach, although certainly not unique by any means, is the importance placed on making sure that interventions into clients' processing of experience are acceptable to them, given that they are reluctant to criticize their counsellors (Rennie, 1994a; Rhodes et al., 1994; Safran, Muran and Wallner Samstag, 1994).

The approach differs from Gendlin's emphasis on focusing and from the process-experiential approach, however, in that the process work it entails is less technical (and, by the same token, is closer in this respect to Toukmanian's approach). In this sense it has kinship with the non-technical work of the literalists. At the same time, as indicated, it lays the groundwork for the technical work of the experiential and process-experiential therapists, should someone trained in it wish to incorporate those techniques.

Experience and its leading edge

Rogers (1959) has defined experience as everything that is in awareness and potentially available for awareness. More fitting is the concept of experiencing as a felt-meaning, or felt-sense, which was a notion that Rogers gradually came to use under Gendlin's influence, and one that is very much in keeping with Rogers's practice of therapy. Incongruence then becomes more clearly a matter of inaccurate symbolization of experience.

The felt-sense is the leading edge (Gendlin, 1981) of the client's experience. When the client and therapist are fully and actively engaged in following the client's leading edge, the client's experience is one of directional movement in the pursuit of meaning and the resolution of troubling feelings. Catching the edge of the client's experience and following that lead is foremost in the current approach. As with the practice of person-centred counsellors who emphasize therapist congruence and its expression – counsellors like Mearns, Thorne and Lietaer – the approach encourages counsellors to communicate their inner experience if it seems appropriate. This deliberate, discretionary expression of the internal experience is more interpersonal and existential than is characteristic of the literal person-centred approach as typically practised. This expression of congruence is also similar to the empathic engagement practised by the process-experiential group, and it is very much like Gendlin's use of his experience of himself while in relation with the client. Such approaches differ from the present one, however, because of its emphasis on metacommunication, or communication about communication (cf. Kiesler, 1996).

Holism

For reasons that are mysterious, we seem to 'be' an 'I' and a 'me', and there seems to be an intrinsic and dynamic relationship between them. There are all sorts of difficulties associated with this notion from a philosophical point of view. The concepts of the individual and of personal identity are considered by some to be Western and to have a surprisingly short history, arising at the onset of the Enlightenment (Taylor, 1989). In this vein, the distinction between the 'I' and the 'me', which was made by James ([1890] 1950) and Mead (1934), originated with Kant's contrast between the transcendental and empirical egos. In any case, the 'I' is the 'executive' that directs attention and forms intentions. Its nature is beyond our grasp because there is no 'ultra-I' to observe it. On the other hand, the 'me' is our sense of ourselves when our 'I' directs our attention to our thoughts and feelings about ourselves – it is our sense of identity.

The concepts of the 'I' and 'me' have come under attack by behaviourists, language philosophers, connectionists and postmodernists alike. It is argued that the concepts are thoroughly modern legacies of Cartesian dualism, Romanticism and Rousseau's humanism, and are mere metaphors. This may be so but I think that it is incontestable that the concepts capture our (admittedly Westernized) *experience* of ourselves. Rogers was led to the same conclusion during the development of his thought. He began by discounting the concept of self (like Dewey) but was led back to it when encountering repeated references to it by his clients (Rogers, 1959).

Related to our sense of the 'I' and 'me', we cherish the sense, whether illusory or not, that we are free to make choices regarding ourselves, our lives. We resist determinisms in the form of reductions of all sorts, believing that we are more than drives, neural nets, schemas, templates or programmes.

The point is, although the concept of self is modernist it is not outdated. It is compatible with the post-postmodernist thinking addressed above to the effect that human beingness is incarnated embodiment and cannot be reduced. Yet this is an embodiment *in* the world, not separate from it. It thus includes cultural forms and language and the relativism that this immersion implies.[7] This sentiment runs throughout the book. The result is an approach that expresses the humanism of Rogers and the literalists but in terms of an ontology that, I believe, more coherently connects the individual with the world (including social relations); it thus presupposes social constructionism to a greater extent (but not exclusively by any means) than is true of Rogerian humanism. It is also very much in keeping with Gendlin's view that the felt-sense is holistic and that human beingness is far more complex than is grasped by all the theories combined.

The present approach is less compatible with the information-processing model adopted by the process-experientialists and Toukmanian. The reductionism of the information-processing model inclines its adherents to reify schemes as agents. The metaphor of schemes is useful because it reminds us that experience occurs within frames of reference. Something is lost, however, when this way of looking at experience eclipses reflexivity. Instead, the presupposition underlying what follows is that we have cognitive/affective structures, undergo non-reflexive processing *and* are reflexive as well.

Summary

The current approach to counselling has been influenced strongly by a research enquiry into the client's reported moment-to-moment experiencing of counselling, which has led to the highlighting of reflexivity, defined as self-awareness and agency within that self-awareness. It is maintained that this quality of human beingness accounts for much of the experience and activity of both clients and counsellors. In turn, the recognition that human experience is non-reflexive as well as reflexive opens the door to the characterization of all people as patients as well as agents.

The counselling approach worked out within this theory thus draws upon existential therapy and interpersonal therapy in support of its deepest promptings which are very much in keeping with the respect for the agency and dignity of the client characteristic of literal person-centred counselling. Its recognition that no one is in a position to be free from non-reflexive entanglements introduces a shift in the structure of power in the counselling relationship, however. In the current approach, it is maintained that clients may have to draw upon the counsellor's agency for a while until they can become sufficiently agential on their own. This proposition thus opens the door to the utility of guiding clients in how to work with their experience, and affiliates the approach with the various experiential therapies.

Notes

1. While preparing this book I have been made aware through Habermas ([1968] 1971) that this definition of reflexivity is supported by Fichte's concept of self-reflection as action that returns to itself.
2. Apart from her concern about Gendlin's dualism; see below.
3. This limitation may have applied more to his theory than his practice, however. Zimring (1990) claims that, contrary to common opinion, Rogers reflected clients' reactions to their feelings more than the feelings themselves. A *reaction to* a feeling is reflexive, a 'mind looking at itself', and is dualistic in this sense.
4. Gendlin compounds the issues (see Sass, 1988) raised by his claim that the felt-sense is a direct referent or exact form when he attempts to reconcile the subjectivity of experiencing with the objectivism of natural science (see Gendlin, 1962). In support of his notion of the direct referent as preconceptual and *available for* symbolization, he declares that the direct referent is *real*, which is fair enough. He also recognizes its amenability to alternative interpretations, which introduces relativism, and which is also sound. Nevertheless, he appears reluctant to accept that the realism and relativism can be reconciled methodically, seemingly because of his desire to hold on to positivism. Attempting to integrate method with philosophical hermeneutics rather than keeping it separate from it makes it somewhat easier to reconcile realism and relativism methodically (see Rennie, 1998).
5. Brodley (1990) argues that Gendlin's focusing technique promotes 'it' language rather than 'I' language. When Gendlin directs clients to attend to feelings, his use of 'it' language to heighten awareness in this regard does tend to leave a mind–body residue, but I see that as an artifact of his technique rather than an expression of his ontology. In any case, as will be seen, the present approach is not subject to the same criticism.
6. It can be argued that Rogers was deeply incoherent when trying to adhere to a unitary concept of organism while trying to work with the concept of self. His organismic unity is very similar to Dewey's concept of monistic naturalism. Yet, when differentiating between an 'organismic self' and a 'social self' he introduced a dualism.
7. The term 'post-postmodernist' is being used to convey the attempt to reconcile modernism and postmodernism (see, for example, Margolis, 1986, 1987).

2
The Client as Agent

Like everyone, clients are both patients and agents. Moreover, their agency is entailed in their reflexivity, just as it is in counsellors. In order to realize that persons are reflexively agential in this way, all we have to do is to turn our attention to ourselves. We then become aware that somehow we have done just that – turned attention to ourselves; we realize that in some mysterious way we have the ability to do this. In this activity we may focus on any aspect that we bring into awareness pertaining to our past (including the 'present', which is really the immediate past) or our future. Within this focus, we have feelings associated with whatever it is we are attending to and these feelings influence what we do next. Some kinds of feelings beckon us further into the thoughts in which we find ourselves and we attend further to them. Alternatively, the feelings associated with a given thought or line of thought may be disturbing in some way, in which case we may be chary of such thoughts, perhaps even turning away from them or altering them in some way to ease the feelings. Moreover, we have the option of engaging in thoughts and feelings only, or of behaving as well. We can lie in bed, thinking and feeling that we should get up, or we can also actually arise. In therapy, we can think and feel something, or we can say it as well – even act it – depending on our preference.

The pursuit of meaning

In the main, in the counselling hour, clients focus on themselves (Phillips, 1984, 1985). That is why they are there; it is their hour, a time when they can concentrate exclusively on themselves without feeling guilty about it. In their active self-focus, their thoughts are pulled in the direction of their inner disturbances. Even though they might not be able to specify exactly what they are searching for, they have a sense of being on a path, or track (Gendlin, 1974, 1996; Pearson, 1974; Rennie, 1990; Wexler, 1974). The path is often unclear, especially at the outset of attention to it. However, as they get more in contact with it, associations, memories and feelings flow into it and they move more deeply into themselves. In this state, their experience is highly internalized; they are hardly aware of their surroundings and may be only dimly aware of the counsellor.

This is not say that even in such moments the counsellor is unnecessary. Clients are helped along their paths when presenting them in the presence of an attentive listener more than when only thinking them. Somehow, the act of expression enlivens the path. It is likely it has a lot to do with clients hearing themselves as they talk. Actually saying what one is thinking and feeling is an externalization, a projection into the world. It is realized that it really *was* said, that it really *did* come from oneself and perhaps *is* a part of oneself. Moreover, the path is even further enlivened when, in hearing themselves speak, they have the sense that what they have just said is all right. This is why it is better to express thoughts in the presence of others, depending on how others receive what is said. And so when counsellors accept without recrimination their clients' utterances, clients' sense of the legitimacy of what they have said is confirmed, which is encouraging. A counsellor may convey this acceptance even when being silent, depending on whether or not the client seems to want a response, and on the counsellor's facial expression and other subtle body language in that moment. Alternatively, the counsellor may respond. When this occurs, the response may signal to the client that what has just been said is understood and acceptable, which deepens the same sense conveyed by the non-verbal indicators given by the therapist. Moreover, the counsellor's response may have extra meaning in it which, if coincidental in some way with the client's track, may have the effect of stimulating in the client still more associations, memories and feelings, thus prompting further progress along the path.

Whether we are clients or not, when we are intently on a path, there may be long moments of non-reflexivity during which we are not aware of what we are thinking or saying *as such* but instead are caught up in thinking or talking. The qualification has to do with feeling. As we non-reflexively think or talk we nevertheless have a feeling-sense of the significance of what we are doing. It is this sense that gives us direction; we know through it the point we have reached now in terms of where we want to go. Moreover, our feelings may have to do with a sense of alarm, depending on where we have got to in our thoughts, or seem about to go with them. We thus have a 'fringe' (as William James put it) of feeling coincident with our thinking and acting that guides us as we go.

This non-reflexive experiencing, guided by the fringe of feeling, proceeds until whatever we intended comes to an end, until affect rises in us to such an extent that we break out of the non-reflexive path, or until our path is disturbed by an interference from outside that captivates our attention. In all such cases the movement along the path comes to a halt, and we attend to where we are at within ourselves and decide what to do next. This is the moment of explicit self-awareness that is the juncture between lines of thought; it is the reflexive moment (Rennie, 1997).

The flowing in and out of non-reflexive and reflexive experiencing, as defined in this way, is more complicated when we are engaged in conversation because the presence and activity of the other person greatly influence our feelings as we engage a path. This is especially the case when the path is pursued in earnest and in which the stakes are high, as in counselling. When clients converse with their counsellor, they are keenly aware of whether or not the counsellor is prepared to listen to them, understand them, accept them. These accountings influence clients' inclinations to follow their paths. The renderings also influence how much clients feel they can safely tell the counsellor *as* they follow their paths. They are sensitive to the counsellor's facilitation or derailment of the train of thought. Facilitation is experienced as a hit on target and the resulting joy can be considerable, although not necessarily expressed. Alternatively, derailing is distressing and puts clients in a dilemma. They would like to ignore the counsellor and to continue on their path; sometimes they actually do so (Rennie, 1990, 1992, 1994b, 1994c). More characteristically, however, they suspend their movement along on the path and turn their attention to the intervention. While doing this, they are torn between pursuing their train of thought and embarking on a new one in response to the counsellor. This is a moment of tension because they are afraid that they are going to lose the thread of their own thought. If the thread happens to be one that has been elusive and difficult to grasp, the prospect of losing it is especially disturbing. Regardless of the tension associated with the forced abandonment of a thread of thought, clients experience relief when, at the end of their interventions, counsellors bring clients back on track.

Deference to the counsellor

Attention is given to counsellors even though they are off-base because clients are, typically, highly deferential. My enquiry into the client's experience of counselling/therapy suggests that there are a number of reasons for this deference (Rennie, 1994a). First, clients see themselves as lay people and their counsellors as wise experts when it comes to the matter of counselling. Hence, clients tend to mistrust their judgements when they conflict with those of the counsellor. Second, clients are afraid to criticize their counsellors. As much as they trust counsellors, they are aware that counsellors, like anyone else, must have their own insecurities. They are afraid that criticism might be resented and cause the counsellor to pull away or to hold it against them in some way. Third, rather than challenging, they prefer to try to ascertain where the counsellor is 'coming from' so that they will be able to attune both their way of looking at things and their discourse to the counsellor's frame of reference. Fourth, they try to meet the counsellor's expectations in the interest of being a good client. Fifth, they realize that counsellors are people like anyone else (despite the attribution of extraordinary wisdom to them) and cannot be expected to be perfect; consequently they accept counsellors' limitations so long as they manage to do some good. Sixth, although wishing that they could talk to the counsellor about what they experience as difficulties in their communication with him or her, they are very reluctant to initiate such metacommunication because they feel that to do so would be to reverse roles. Seventh, if it should happen that the counselling is subsidized, they feel that they have no right to complain because 'beggars cannot be choosers'. Lastly, in rare instances, unwelcome pressure to comply with the counsellor's direction may become so great that clients are moved to attack the counsellor but, even here, the attack is indirect (for example, by subtly threatening the counsellor's self-esteem; Rennie, 1994b) and the client beats a hasty retreat.

Among these properties of deference, perhaps the most surprising one, especially for beginning counsellors, is the client's forgiveness of mistakes. Contrary to what counsellors may expect of themselves, clients do not expect them to be on target every time (see also Gendlin, 1996). Clients instead generally feel that, so long as the counsellor is helpful more often than not, the overall counselling is useful and it would be in poor taste to rub the counsellor's nose in his or her mistakes. In this regard, there is room for the counsellor to relax about mistakes – at least with most clients. On the other hand, the reverse of this forgiveness and corresponding silence about the counsellor's errors is that the client's experience of therapy is not necessarily as positive as the client leads the counsellor to believe. In the main, then, for most clients in most therapy sessions, there are periods of productive work interspersed with non-productive or even negative periods that are charitably written off.

An instance of a client's weathering of a rupture in a generally good therapy relationship was given by one of the participants in my study (see Box 2.1).

Box 2.1
An instance of a client's deferential management of a momentary rupture in the relationship with the counsellor

A participant ('Amy') in my research into the client's experience of a counselling session described herself as being burdened with self-pity. She disclosed that in a counselling session that had preceded the one we were studying she had wanted to get to the bottom of why she was so self-pitying. In reply, her counsellor (who was usually non-directive and always supportive) had suggested that that wouldn't lead anywhere and that it would be better for Amy to accept her self-pity and work from there. Amy had remembered this earlier event when in the counselling session under study. She indicated that, throughout this current session, she had wanted to go back to the question of why she was self-pitying but had felt inhibited because of her counsellor's admonition. Hence, according to her report, Amy had operated on two levels in the session. One had involved going with the flow of the discourse with her counsellor, while the other had entailed thinking about the 'Why?' question. In being discursive, the first level had been overt (apart from whatever covert, reflexive activity had been involved in it), whereas the second level had been entirely covert and private.

The reports of other participants in this study indicate that clients are capable of using their counselling for their own purposes when it is unsatisfactory in some way (as Bohart [1997] put it, they make lemonade out of lemons).

Example

Another young woman ('Betty'; pseudonyms are used throughout the book) declared that, in her first few counselling sessions, she hadn't liked the fact that her counsellor had reflected what she had been saying. She had wanted his personal reactions to her concerns. After feeling dissatisfied about his approach during the first four meetings, she had finally told him what she had felt. She had been gratified to find that after that he had loosened up and had occasionally shared something of himself.

After arousing his personal side and knowing that one of her main problems was difficulty in trusting her own judgement, she decided to present to the counsellor three interpersonal events that she had experienced during the previous week, each having required social judgement. She planned to test her social judgement in the situations against the counsellor's reactions to them. Without letting him in on the plan, she presented each incident in turn and, each time, elicited from him an opinion on the appropriate course of action, without letting him know what *her* choice had been. She delightedly informed me that his judgement had coincided with her own in all three instances and that, after the third concordance, she had felt enormously strengthened.

These examples depict accommodation to counselling when what the counsellor does is not in keeping with what the client wants. As indicated, depending on the strength of the deference, the client may either suffer in silence or (less commonly) actually let the counsellor know of the concern in a bid to influence the latter's approach. Surrounding and infusing such disjunctions is the relationship as a whole with the counsellor. When the relationship is mainly positive, such adjustments are integrated into an overall working alliance (see Chapter 9). Clients are surprisingly accommodating when faced with a deficiency of some sort in the counselling, especially when it is experienced as beneficial overall. They may decide not to attempt to deal with a given concern when the counsellor indicates in one way or another that he or she either cannot or does not want to deal with it, and proceed to deal with it on their own.

Power struggles

The lack of fit between what clients want and what the counsellor delivers can become serious. Clients may find themselves in power struggles in that they are exhorted to change in particular directions that they secretly and ardently feel are inappropriate. In other instances the counsellor may appear to clients to be meeting his or her own needs. When this happens, clients often feel precarious because they are preoccupied with the counsellor's judgement.

Thus, when disjunctions of this severity occur, they often become for clients the primary, but private, theme of the counselling. The saliency of this theme undermines the extent to which they can engage in productive self-focus, unless they can privately and creatively derive implications of the theme for their relationships with people outside the relationship with the counsellor. In any case, clients in this situation find that they are spending as much time and energy, if not more, managing their relationship with their counsellor as they spend on their relationship with themselves. To complicate matters further, the difficulty with the relationship with the counsellor tends to contaminate everything that he or she does.

An example illustrating such a power struggle was given by another participant in my study.

Example

'Audrey' was a woman in her early twenties who was having trouble with her family, especially her mother. She was being seen by a woman counsellor who was inclined toward a feminist approach, supported by the use of gestalt techniques. Audrey's view was that her difficulties lay not so much with her as with the family, whereas she got the impression that her counsellor held the opposite view. She wanted to work with Audrey's feelings about the family, whereas the latter wanted some practical help on how to deal with it. In this vein, the counsellor had asked Audrey to write her autobiography, due three weeks from the time of assignment. Audrey had been worried because, of late, her work on the assignment had tailed off. The relationship with the counsellor was such that Audrey had been unable to tell her this, however, and she had dreaded the unpleasantness of having to admit it if confronted.

In these circumstances, the way she handled the matter was inventive and reveals the lengths to which clients may go in order to protect their dignity when dealing with a counsellor who threatens it.

Shortly into the session, there was a pause in which Audrey worried that the counsellor might remember the assignment. Knowing that the counsellor liked to work with dreams, Audrey introduced one to 'head the counsellor off at the pass'. In fact, mused Audrey (to me, the researcher), she may have *had* the dream just so that she could use it for this purpose. In any case, the manoeuvre worked. The counsellor never got round to asking about the autobiography. (For the discourse as well as Audrey's commentary on it, see Rennie, 1997.)

Thus, clients often struggle for power while not wanting to challenge the counsellor directly and so must resort to other ways of exerting their power. What Audrey further revealed about what had ensued after the disclosure of the dream depicts how, within a tenuous working alliance, everything the counsellor does is in danger of being contaminated by the client's lack of trust and goodwill.

The dream was about Christmas morning. Under the tree Audrey had a gift with the price tag still on it. It said the gift was worth $10. Yet, when opened, the gift proved be a chintzy spice rack, certainly not worth $10. The counsellor had asked Audrey to role-play *being* the price tag. She had been very sceptical about this task. She explained to me that, although she was a drama major, she had never been asked to dramatize anything as inanimate as a price tag on a gift. Nevertheless, she had made a go of it. At a certain point, in the role, she had made a remark to the effect that the value on the outside did not reflect the true value on the inside. The counsellor had seized upon this sentence, asking Audrey to repeat it. It was only after the third repetition that she had grasped its significance for her sense of herself. She reported that she prided herself in knowing what she was about to say but that this sentence had slipped out, beyond her control. In response, she had admired the counsellor's cleverness in getting round her defence in this way and *yet begrudged it at the same time*.

So, rather than feeling that she and the counsellor had been partners in a common quest, Audrey had felt more like a competitor with the counsellor. Moreover, the way in which she reported this reaction gave the strong impression that, by virtue of this competition, she was prevented from fully owning the insight (conceptualizing within the framework of existential psychotherapy; May [1958a] explains this beautifully by suggesting that, in such a circumstance, the client's relationship with the insight is contaminated). Yet, in the light of the outcome of her intervention, the counsellor had every right to believe that they had been working in concert and successfully as well.

Summary

Clients may unreflexively be at one with their discourse and behaviour. Alternatively, they may monitor and control both their discourse and how they behave generally in the therapy interaction. When operating reflexively in this way, they may deliberately say what they feel they need to and should say in some instances, withhold what they are experiencing in others, and distort or deny what they are thinking and feeling in still others. They may carry on a private therapeutic discourse that is concurrent with the dialogue with the counsellor, using the latter as a catalyst for the former. They may discriminate between beneficial and non-beneficial contributions by the counsellor, respond intensely to the former and politely go through the motions of working with the latter. Moreover, they may do all this so smoothly that it may be difficult for the counsellor to detect negative appraisals.

When counsellors are interested non-judgementally in their clients and are open to their experience, it helps clients to work productively with experience, reflexively monitored and guided or not. This is especially true for clients who are reasonably comfortable with their experience and are accustomed to working symbolically with it. Depending on the individual, however, contact with experience and learning how to work even more productively is expedited when counsellors take advantage of monitoring of their experience of the client's experience and act in terms of the returns from that monitoring, as seems fit. By the same token, the work of counselling may be expedited when counsellors invite clients to pay attention to how they are working with their experience and/or guide them in how they might do so more productively.

The first way of being with clients is in keeping with the literal approach to person-centred counselling, while the second way expresses the experiential approach in a general sense. In Chapter 3, consideration is given to clients' and counsellors' expectations surrounding the opening counselling session. The chapter is thus preliminary to the actual activity of counselling and has to do with the kinds of considerations that the counsellor might take into account that may help him or her to become empathic, unconditionally positively regarding and congruent. In Chapter 4 and the chapters that follow we address the actual task of counselling.

3
The First Meeting

Clients and counsellors are often nervous about their first meeting. Clients entering counselling for the first time have made a momentous decision. It is not easy to admit that one cannot take care of oneself. Many people agonize for a long time before taking such a step and often go through many false starts. As the day arrives, preoccupations and worries rise to the surface and clients wonder: 'Who is to say that my problems are important enough to warrant counselling? What if the counsellor doesn't take me seriously?' Or, 'How did I get into this state? I can't believe that I'm actually contemplating seeing someone. I'm used to solving problems on my own.' Or, 'What if I get someone who won't listen to me, or even laughs at me? I couldn't stand that.' Or, 'What am I getting myself into? Once I get hooked up with a counsellor, will I be trapped?' Or, 'What if it doesn't work out with this person? It's taken so much effort to work up to the decision to go to her, I don't think I could start over again with someone else.' Or, 'What if he decides that he doesn't want to see me but refers me to somebody else?'

Seasoned clients tend to worry more about who they will be seeing, their anxieties centring on this relationship: 'I sure hope that this person spends more time with me than the last one did.' Or, 'I hope that this person isn't as wrapped up in himself as the last one was.' Or, 'I hope this counsellor will give more of herself than the other one did. She never talked about herself. I always felt that she was distant and cold when I was with her. I never knew who she was as a person.' Naturally, these kinds of thoughts do not exclude self-focused thoughts, entailing resolutions to work harder and so on.

Counsellors have their own worries. Beginning counsellors are tormented by their inexperience and feelings of inadequacy, wondering 'What do I do if I get something I can't handle? Do I run out of the room looking for my supervisor? How will I be able to do that and preserve any semblance of competence?' Or, 'What if I get someone who affects me so much that I lose control?' Or, 'What if this person won't talk?' Or, 'What if she accuses me of being too young?' It is easy for beginning counsellors to work themselves into a frenzy with such thoughts.

Experienced counsellors have their worries too. Often these revolve around concerns about energy, commitment, known limitations, and impressions of the seriousness of the new client's difficulties. Thoughts like these often run through their minds: 'I'm not sure I have either the interest or energy to give another client what he needs.' Or, 'On the phone, she sounded like she could be pretty clingy. I'm not sure I'm up to dealing with another overly dependent client at present.' The chances are that these kinds of thoughts will remain private as the client and counsellor meet. This being the case, it is useful for us to remind ourselves that clients usually come in with many doubts and uncertainties about the counselling undertaking, in addition to the personal concerns that make up the explicit subject matter of the first session. Maintaining our awareness of the overall context predisposes us to be alert to unexpressed conflicts that the client may be experiencing.

How can we promote making a positive impact on the client during the first meeting? Keeping in mind the realization that clients are agents in their own right contributes to several attitudes that can ease the pressure.

Counsellor attitudes promoting an initial positive impact on clients

Taking the long view

It is useful to remind ourselves that, with the possible exception of acute crises, we need not feel obliged immediately to remediate the client's problems. Many beginning counsellors are overwhelmed by the distress that the client is experiencing and want to dive in and resolve things right away. Yet clients do not necessarily expect a quick solution. It is often the case that the same problems, in one form or another, have been experienced for years. Indeed, clients' identities may be defined in terms of the problems in many respects (Bohart and Tallman, 1996) and they may be reluctant to let go of them. The existential uncertainty experienced when change is anticipated is often more disturbing than staying the same. In any case, in the absence of a crisis, the counsellor has lots of room to relax.

Reining in the impulse to effect change

It helps to realize that clients may want comfort more than change in the early stage of counselling (Noble, 1986). Comfort comes from two sources. In the main, it is achieved through the opportunity to talk because, through talk, things become clearer and feelings can be expressed. It is the expression of feelings, particularly, that provides relief. People often have to turn to counsellors to do this because friends and relatives get tired of listening. More fundamentally, friends and relatives have difficulty listening without either distancing and diminishing the person's problems or getting too close and giving advice.

Comfort also involves hope. Clients and beginning counsellors sometimes get out of step with each other because of differing senses of the importance of time. Inexperienced counsellors often become caught up in the intensity of the client's distress and want to resolve it quickly to give relief. Clients, on the other hand, being aware that they have had their problems for lengthy periods of time, are more interested in getting a sense of whether or not they will ever get relief. To put it another way, the counsellor may perceive anxiety whereas the client may be more in tune with despair. The prospect of relief over the long term can be comforting to clients. It is as much as they could have hoped for from an initial counselling session.

The opposite can be true, as well, of course. Some clients want an answer *now*, or so they say. Such a demand puts pressure on the counsellor and the impulse to try to deliver may be strong; nevertheless, it is best to resist such entreaties. In the first place, it is difficult to meet such demands so early on because the counsellor cannot know enough about the client to make a proper assessment of the prospect of change (even if the counsellor were prepared to share with the client such an assessment in any case, which is another matter). To attempt to meet this demand would, therefore, get things off on the wrong foot. Moreover, it is paradoxical but true that counsellors who resist quick solutions often stimulate a sense of hope, even in clients who are desperate, because such an assessment is realistic – and also subtly implies that the achievement of greater goals may be possible further on down the line. Alternatively, counsellors who try to accomplish a great deal in the first session may stimulate scepticism.

The locus of responsibility

It also reduces pressure on counsellors when we allow ourselves to realize that, ultimately, it is the responsibility of the clients themselves to come to grips with their problems. This attitude can be maintained only if we believe they have the capacity, potentially, to deal with them. As indicated, to the extent that clients seem to be patients in the face of their difficulties, a certain amount of scepticism in this regard is justified. The challenge is not to make clients into patients when it is not warranted. It may be difficult to keep in mind that most clients are both patients and agents; after all, we categorize reality in order to simplify it. Moreover, this tendency is made even more compelling when we have the need to feel competent at all times. We can feel that way, especially, if we cast ourselves in the role of expert, and it is thus tempting to think of ourselves as the only agent in the counselling room. When doing this, we lose sight of the client's responsibility and, in turn, increase the pressure that we put on ourselves.

On one level, clients may love it when we become experts. This may be what they came for: to have someone provide answers and solve problems. Given the chance, they pummel us with difficult questions and demands, backing us into a corner. On another level, clients know that they need to play a major, if not the major, role in solving their problems; thus when we dive in and attempt to assume responsibility, their relief is mixed with doubt about whether or not that will prove fruitful in the long run. Also, clients may perversely love it when we assume control because it gives them a chance to experience their own power by thwarting our efforts. Consequently, our exercise of power is better directed toward mobilizing clients' power. Beyond that, should we assume more direct control, it is best done in the context of active negotiation with our clients, within and contributing to the working alliance.

Objectifying the client

I find it helpful to try to refrain from reacting either positively or negatively to clients and instead to try to be interested in them. Letting go of evaluation is not always easy; we have spent our lives being evaluational of people. As we meet new people, we subconsciously appraise them in terms of people we have known. We also have ideals of people that are mixtures of real people from our past and fantasized people whom we have never met, and new people may be evaluated in terms of such ideals as well, whether we are aware of it or not. It takes effort to detach ourselves from these predisposing emotional entanglements and to react to clients impartially. Moreover, counselling is hard work. It seems almost natural to develop opinions about the extent to which clients will be 'easy to work with'.

The difficulty posed by negative appraisals is that they may interfere with our ability to listen to clients. When we evaluate clients negatively, the appraisals have a tendency to spill over into our judgements about what they say. We set up a tendency to under-perceive some of the content of what clients tell us. This can lead to 'spotty' listening. Worse, it may make us disinclined to penetrate beneath the surface of what they convey. It is much more pleasant to be simply interested in clients, to view them as wonderfully complex – so complex that they will never be fully fathomed, just as we are so complex that we cannot fully fathom ourselves. If we approach the situation in this way it is easier to be open to predispositions that may be compellingly influencing clients to be the ways they are.

When I mention this thought about detachment to beginning counsellors, I sense that I am often perceived as being cold and clinical. I do not mean to imply that in adopting an attitude of detached interest we are not caring for clients. I am trying to distinguish between caring in the sense that we are deeply interested in clients' welfare and caring as an over-identification with clients' problems. The early assumption of a heavy mantle of care has always seemed to me as if the person caring feels that caring, if deep enough, will make clients whole. My view is that such caring is supported by an implicit belief that clients cannot help themselves, from an underlying lack of appreciation of clients' agency and correspondingly from a premature mistrust of their capacity for control.

In suggesting interested detachment, I do not mean to imply that we should deny our subjectivity. Far from it. Our subjectivity often resonates with clients' experiences. The trick is to know when our subjectivity is a resonation and when simply a projection of our own unresolved issues. Moreover, our experience of the *relationship* with the client may be brought out into the open usefully at times, and especially if it is in crisis (these considerations are addressed in later chapters). Thus, in productive, interested detachment, we are subjectively involved but are also detached from that involvement, which means that we can take it or leave it, depending on what seems right for the client in the given moment. This is my understanding of what the term 'empathy' means.

Tolerating ambiguity

The last attitude that I shall address is partly an attitude and partly a cognitive skill. I am referring to our ability to tolerate ambiguity. Clients are not only complex, in many cases they seem hopelessly so. As they spin their webs of mystery we get increasingly entangled in false trails, contradictions and a general lack of direction. Everything seems out of control. Furthermore, all of this usually occurs in a context of urgency. It is tempting to dive in to make sense of the mess, to create some sort of cognitive closure. This is where the lay person's tendency to give advice comes into play. We may feel the same impulse, or at least that we want to structure things at the end of the session in order to give the client a sense of control. It makes us feel uncomfortable to allow a session to end with everything up in the air. It is easy to forget that if we succumb to the desire to create closure by giving advice or interpreting, chances are we will be doing the same thing as the clients' relatives and friends have done. We lose sight of the fact that if such efforts were useful then the client would never have needed to come to us in the first place.

There is an additional complication. Should we allow ourselves to feel responsible for closure, then we must be busy at creating it. This in turn means that in such moments we have been engaged in two trains of thought: one to do with listening to the client and the other devoted to coming up with answers. Because it is impossible to think two things at once, we move back and forth between the two trains of thought. We do our evaluative thinking in the pauses between the client's utterances, during boring discourse by the client or – worst of all – even during what is, in fact, important discourse, if only we had heard it. This is thus yet another cause of spotty listening.

I am not convinced that doing counselling in this way does much good. We lose sight of the fact that clients are just as busy at evaluating their material as we are. They have two trains of thought as well. Moreover, they pay more attention to their evaluations than to ours, should we decide to share our appraisals. In addition, the politics of the counselling relationship predisposes clients to give the appearance of agreeing with us, regardless of their inner conviction. Unfortunately, we may thus be inappropriately reinforced. This is not to say that interpretations are not truly valued by clients. Elliott et al. (1985) have shown that, when asked to identify the most significant moments in counselling, clients often report on moments within which the counsellor gave an interpretation. These were seasoned counselling relationships, however, and the interpretations were well timed.

Especially in the early stage, it is better to move into the flow of the client's world and to be carried along with it, even though it involves a lot of ambiguity. As we shall see shortly, this going with the flow does not exclude interventions designed to highlight clients' experiencing of themselves. However, it does mean that we actively inhibit the impulse to derive a structure and to offer it to the client. In part, clients may be disappointed by our refusal to structure. Yet, at a deeper level, they may fear truth about themselves. They may be afraid that they are going to be *found out* by us. This fear is usually secret; it is their hope that they more easily reveal to us. Consequently we are perhaps being naïve when sensing that there is pressure to structure and only that. I find the best way to approach clients' demands for structure is to convey to them that, although things may not seem very clear at this stage, this does not necessarily mean that they will not become clear later on. Putting it this way lets me off the hook while providing a basis for hope. It is also honest. We can be reasonably confident in promising clarity because, as bewildering as clients' content may be at the outset, it usually becomes thematic if we listen long enough. Themes that became evident in this way are usually embedded in the client's experience. Hence, any efforts we may then make to represent the structure of it have a greater chance of being assimilated than is the case if we attempt to structure before the themes have become apparent.

The matter of informed consent

When people enter into a counselling relationship, they have a right to know what they are letting themselves in for before consenting to the course of counselling. They need to know about such matters as the fee, if involved, and acceptable methods of payment; the use of taping, if it is to be involved; and any potential adverse effects of the counselling including, especially, any limits to confidentiality.

Some matters requiring informed consent are specified as standards of professional conduct by regulatory bodies. To the extent that they are made part of the statutory regulations governing the practice of the profession, they become law. Limits to confidentiality, on the other hand, are often a matter of law regardless of professional regulation.

Not all counsellors are regulated. In most jurisdictions, terms such as 'counsellor' and 'therapist' are not statutory, unlike the terms 'psychologist', 'psychology' and 'psychological', or some combination of them. But even if counsellors are not regulated, they must still uphold the law. Thus, depending on whether or not the counsellor is regulated, the range of matters requiring informed consent may vary but the chances are it will invariably include limits to confidentiality. For example, in the United Kingdom and most, if not all, jurisdictions in North America, the communication between the client and a counsellor is not privileged. This means that a counsellor may be called by subpoena to testify in court regarding what he or she knows about a given client, and/or to turn over to the court his or her records. In recognition of the importance of confidentiality in counselling/psychotherapy a judge may be reluctant to impose a break in confidentiality upon the counsellor/therapist (I am told that in Great Britain this consideration particularly applies to marital counselling/therapy). Similarly, the judge may, when considering the relevance of a therapist's records which have been subpoenaed, decide on the admissability of the records, whole or in part, to the court. In the United Kingdom, all such decisions are made at the judge's discretion, not by rule. In Canada, such case law has recently been made statutory, but only with respect to counselling/therapy involving the treatment of sexual abuse. Moreover, as this book goes to press, the constitutionality of this law is under question, on the grounds that it violates the rights granted to the defendant under the Canadian Charter of Rights and Freedoms. Finally, in a related domain, it is true of many jurisdictions that reasonable grounds for suspicion that an individual has engaged in child abuse must, under law, be conveyed to the authorities.

Having to acquire informed consent to counselling makes some counsellors feel uneasy, especially in the opening session. They prefer to give clients free rein to tell their stories and to pour out their feelings. It seems an interference to have to inform clients about the implications of entering into counselling. Moreover, it seems especially disruptive to have to inform clients about the limits of confidentiality. Counsellors can easily worry that having to do this will discourage clients from entering counselling. Yet it must be done.

One way to do it is to prepare a form that gives the necessary information and to have clients study it in advance of the first meeting, and sign it. At the outset of the first meeting, the counsellor can check with the client to make sure that the form was read and understood and then proceed with the session. Alternatively, we may decide to inform clients during the first meeting and have them sign the consent form at that time. In this approach, the information is best given at the very outset of the session, with an opening such as, 'Before we begin, there are a number of things about the prospect of counselling that need to be mentioned.' We then proceed, as lightly as possible but without minimizing what we are saying. We certainly do not want to communicate our anxiety about having to inform them of such matters (especially the limits to confidentiality), causing a contagion effect. The impartation of the necessary information usually takes no more than five minutes. Once made routine, it becomes easier to do.

Summary

Either prior to or at the outset of the first meeting, prospective clients need to be informed about aspects of the counselling that could conceivably affect them in an adverse way and about pertinent housekeeping features of the counselling. Further, the client should sign a form giving consent to the counselling as understood. Once this is done and the session begins, the first encounter with clients is easier if we realize that their problems, typically, have developed over a considerable period of time and will not be remedied overnight; that clients usually want to experience comfort more than to undergo change, especially initially; that the control over clients' experiences belongs in them, not us; that clients are persons stimulating curiosity and not people to be liked or disliked; and that we are about to enter an experience within which we will be bombarded with information which must be kept suspended until patterns begin to emerge.

These beliefs, expectations and attitudes contribute to being prepared to listen them, to be patient with them, to accept them and to have respect for them. These ways of being help to prepare the ground for understanding them and for entering into a productive relationship.

These ways of being are also supportable, to a certain extent, by our style of communicating. The majority of Rogers's responses were reflective, with the remainder usually being checks on whether or not he understood correctly (Miller, 1972). He became concerned when he found that his typical way of responding had become incorporated into a style (Shlien, 1996), however. It was after that realization that he changed the name of his approach from non-directive therapy to client-centred therapy, and began to emphasize therapist congruence because he was tired of defending reflection as a vehicle of empathy (Shlien, 1996; see also Bozarth, 1984). Despite this reaction, however, the fact remains that until the last Rogers adhered to reflective and checking responses because they were in keeping with his style. There is another reason, however: the style promotes staying tight inside the client's frame of reference. What is required is to be able to do this genuinely and meaningfully rather than woodenly and mechanically. To ignore the style because in the wrong hands it can be merely mechanical would be a mistake. So, in the next chapter, we take a closer look at this style and then in succeeding chapters direct our attention to aspects of ourselves that help to make the style our own, and to when the style may not be sufficient.

4
Basic Attending Skills

The term 'basic attending skills' was advanced by Ivey (1971) to describe a number of non-verbal and verbal behaviours that enhance effective listening and communication. In his microcounselling approach to training, Ivey felt that it is easier for counsellors to learn their complex task if their activities are broken into components and worked on one at a time. These skills are ways of keeping close to clients' experience and to let them know that we are interested in them more than in ourselves. Correspondingly, they relate meaningfully to the measurement of the Rogerian core conditions in terms of how that operationalization was worked out by Charles Truax (a student of Rogers) and his associate, Robert Carkhuff, in their model of training person-centred counsellors (e.g. Carkhuff, 1969; Truax and Carkhuff, 1967; for the relationship between the skills and empathy, see Rennie, Burke and Toukmanian, 1978).

As indicated, Rogers had misgivings about any attempt to turn becoming a person-centred counsellor into a matter of learning a certain communication style and perhaps this scepticism influenced the history of the counsellor training movement. Training of this sort flourished only for a decade or so beginning in the late 1960s. Indeed, the shortcoming of this approach to training is that, if not integrated into the counsellor's desire for and actual connection with the client's experience, the focus on style may become independent of that experience. When this happens, the counsellor falls into a mode of implementing the skills regardless of where the client is at – which, of course, is ridiculous. In any event, the skills training approach of this type gave way to a more appropriate focus on attunement and congruence as states of being or attitudes. Coincident with the demise of the movement, the experiential therapists continued to work on their more specialized techniques that are meant to be carried out within the atmosphere of those same attitudes.

I do not mean to turn back the clock when addressing basic attending skills; yet neither do I intend to ignore them because this kind of training is no longer in vogue. There is no reason why the baby should be thrown out with the bath water. The fact of the matter is that there is a style of sorts associated with the person-centred approach and that these attending skills help to define that style. The key is to develop a readiness to enact the style depending on clients' leading edges of experience and on what they seem to need in the moment.

So what are these basic attending skills? In a nutshell, they are non-verbal and verbal behaviours that let clients know that they are the centre of attention. The skills are of two main types: body language and verbal behaviour. Let us look at each of these in turn.

Body language

Clients want us to be interested in them. Thus it is reassuring if we look interested. We may do this in a number of ways but three stand out. First, if we anticipate the session and look forward to it then the positive expectancy will show. Second, eye contact is important, at least to most clients (very shy and/or mistrustful people may feel uncomfortable if we look at them directly a lot). This does not mean that we should stare but we should be capable of looking directly at clients periodically without wavering. As simple as this sounds, it is not easy when we are nervous and insecure. It is almost as if we feel that the eyes really are the windows of the soul. Whatever the reason, it is sometimes difficult to 'look a client straight in the eye' when inwardly we are not sure of what we are doing. If we find ourselves getting into that state as we start with a client, the best thing to do is to force ourselves to establish eye contact. It gets easier once we break the barrier. And the dividends we reap make the effort worth while.

Also, the way we sit is important, especially until clients get to know us. Most practitioners who address this sort of thing advocate the 'forward body lean'. We rest our hands comfortably on our thighs and lean slightly forward – a classic pose of being interested. At the same time, in striking this pose, we would not want to appear catatonic in it.

I continue to be amazed at clients' sensitivity to how we sit. A woman once told me that it was a big day for her when her psychiatrist came out from behind his desk and sat face-to-face with her. (It was also on that day that she noticed that he wore black socks; thereafter she wondered if he would wear another colour – he never did.) One of my own clients disclosed that when I leaned back she had the feeling that I was pulling away from her. I didn't feel that I was, but that was irrelevant; I had behaved in a way that seemed that way to her. Another participant in my research had a similar reaction when her counsellor put her feet up on a chair. The participant remarked:

> Where's her voice? Her voice is back here (motions to the back of her chair). I guess when I really need something, I need someone to lean towards me. I want to feel connected instead of her feet being up on the chair, back like this [demonstrates] – offering a little bit here and there.

In summary, it helps to convey that we are interested in the client when we look forward to a session, are comfortable with eye contact and sit with a forward body lean.

Verbal responses

Lay people who are placed in the role of a counsellor spend most of their time asking fact-finding questions and giving interpretation and advice (Alcorn and Rennie, 1981); this way of responding is negatively correlated with empathy as perceived by raters (Rennie, Burke and Toukmanian, 1978). Beginning counsellors are no exception to this tendency (e.g. Toukmanian and Rennie, 1975). Just why this is so is not especially clear but it probably has a lot to do with the feeling that, when placed in the counsellor role, the person feels called upon to solve the problem. After all, that can easily *seem* to be the structure of such an encounter: the acquaintance comes to the person with a problem and so the natural response is to try to solve it. Even if the acquaintance should insist that all he or she wants is to be listened to, the impulse is still strong to dive in, to ease the pain, to give something that would help.

The mark of the fact-finding, or *closed* question is that it can be answered with a 'Yes' or a 'No'. For example, 'Are you married?' 'Children?' 'Have you been in counselling before?' 'Are you on medication?' 'Do you sleep well at night?' 'Do you have nightmares?' Closed questions serve the purpose of providing the questioner with information. They make up much of the dialogue of a counsellor who, especially in the opening session, is gathering information as part of an assessment, and in this context are legitimate (see Box 4.1). When carried over into counselling, however, unless information extracted by closed questions is considered relevant by clients, having to respond to them is not therapeutic. Such interrogation has more to do with the counsellor's interests than with the client's and – amounting to the same thing – it throws clients off track. Counsellors who discourse in this way in a counselling session have taken it upon themselves to 'figure things out'. They are impatient to understand.

> **Box 4.1**
> **The need for assessment in person-centred counselling**
>
> The need for assessment is generally not emphasized in person-centred counselling. It disrupts clients from focusing on themselves and working with their feelings, shifting the locus of attention from the client to the counsellor. Even so, that does not mean that we should rigidly refuse to assess. One of my favourite stories was told by a colleague who, when teaching a course in assessment-interviewing, scripted an actress to play the role of someone who was concerned about being pregnant. The colleague was amazed to find that the student assigned to interview the woman spent the entire interview exploring her feelings about being pregnant without making any attempt to ascertain if, in fact, she was pregnant. There's a moral here: even though counsellors may not want to burden clients with a barrage of questions which take away from emotional concerns, *some* information may be important and, if it is not volunteered, we need to go after it.

As mentioned earlier, there is evidence that well-timed interpretations are judged by clients in well-established counselling relationships to be among the most useful moments in a given counselling session. Alternatively, there is evidence that attempts to interpret early in counselling are non-empathic, at least in terms of empathy as assessed by raters listening to tapes of counselling sessions. Admittedly, there is a procedural difference involved in these two findings: what clients experience as empathic and what raters judge to be empathic do not necessarily coincide. Given a choice between the two modes of assessment, it makes more sense to respect the client's judgement (Watson, 1984). At the same time the chances are remote that, early on in a counselling relationship, there would have been time to prepare the ground for interpretation, in which case clients in this situation would be likely to react negatively to it.

In the situation of early counselling, then, interpretation stems from the same psychology that leads to the closed question – wanting to solve the problem. The same is even more true of advice-giving. While the closed question gathers information about the problem and interpretation provides an explanation of it, advice advocates a course of action to remediate it. Thus, advice is not only evaluative but prescriptive as well and even more likely to cause resistance.

It is more useful not to give in to the temptation to solve clients' problems and to follow their paths to meaning instead. This is where *verbal following behaviour* (Ivey, 1971; Ivey and Simek-Downing, 1980) or, as the client focused on in Boxes 4.2 and 4.3 described it, 'prompting' comes into play. There are several modes of responding that constitute verbal following behaviour, and these are discussed below.

Minimal encouragements (Ivey, 1971) are supportive remarks such as 'Uh huh', 'Sure', 'Yes, I see', 'Right', 'I'm with you', 'Go on', and so on. These brief utterances are meant to let the client know that we are still there; that even though we are not saying much, we are listening, understanding, accepting. And, of course, how we say such things, including how we look while doing so, mean a lot as well.

Open-ended questions stimulate divergent thinking as opposed to the convergent thinking instigated by the closed question. The former draw the client's attention to a topic while leaving open the client's field of awareness pertaining to it. Hence, when trying to understand the background of what brought the client to counselling, instead of asking a series of closed, information-seeking questions, we may remark, 'I'm gathering that your main concern seems to be you're having trouble settling down to work these days. What are some of the things that seem to be connected with this difficulty?' A query like this, even though disruptive of the flow of clients' dialogue, enables them to draw upon their experience in a way which is meaningful to them. Alternatively, open-ended questions can be used smoothly within the flow as ways of inviting the client to work additionally in some way with what has been said. Questions like, 'How did that strike you?' or 'What did that do for you?' give a flavour of this type of query. Even 'Can you say more about that?', although technically closed, is usually responded to as if it were open. Lastly, open-ended questions may be used as *bids for clarification* when we are confused about what clients are saying. We can be non-abrasive when indicating to clients that they have not been clear when we make queries such, 'Hmm. I've been following you in what you're saying about your difficulties at work, but somehow I didn't quite get how that's tied in with your marriage. I wonder if you could fill that part in a bit more.' The main characteristic of all such open-ended queries is that they invite clients to elaborate on their experience within an open experiential field of awareness.

Open-ended questions make sense to beginning counsellors and are easily assimilated into their response repertoires. *Repetitions* and *paraphrases*, on the other hand, more than any other type of response, seem stupid to beginning counsellors. It is necessary to understand their effect before one can get over this appraisal. As we have seen, the experience of thinking and discourse is such that a person's experience generally seems more real if it is voiced rather than thought. It adds to that reality when it is heard in the voice of another rather than in one's own voice. Hence, when we repeat what the client has said, either directly or in a paraphrase, clients are given mirrors, echoes, of themselves that put them closer in contact with themselves.

Looking at these two types of response more closely, there are important differences between the intent and impact of the repetition and those of the paraphrase, however. The repetition is designed to convey to clients that what they have just said in some way is significant in its own right and that we want to draw their attention to it, to help it sink in. Gendlin is especially aware of this intent and effect. Thus there are moments when, in focusing on their felt-sense, clients seem to have made an accurate symbolization of it – to have come up with the right words. It is Gendlin's experience that, in being accurate, only those words will do, that to say it any other way will detract from the client's experience in that moment. Similarly, to repeat it exactly as it is, and perhaps with an emphasis of various sorts, draws the client's attention to it. It may cause the client to dwell in the experience represented by the words and correspondingly may lead to an association or memory that, when followed, may result in yet another felt-sense, another edge. Thus, regardless of whether or not the felt-sense indeed is a direct referent as opposed to a combination of what the client brings to the interaction with the counsellor and that interaction itself, repeating exactly what the client has said at times is useful because it signals to the client that what was just said is significant, worthy of attention, important. By the same token, it stimulates dwelling within what was said.

The paraphrase comes into play when both the client and the counsellor are within the *zone* of the client's felt-sense but the counsellor does not have the sense that what the client has just said captures it exactly. They are both on the path *to* meaning, groping. In this kind of moment, the counsellor can venture a slight shift in meaning, in keeping with his or her sense of the path, by paraphrasing. The effect is thus subtle. The paraphrase is a safe response in that it stays very much within the client's frame of reference but subtly adds to where the client is at within the frame. If it resonates, then the client picks up the paraphrase and works with it – moves forward a bit. In this way, then, paraphrasing co-constructs the client's experience. As such, even though the counsellor's alterations of what the client has given are slight, in making paraphrases the counsellor influences the client's sense of his or her experience, and paraphrasing should not be treated lightly by either the counsellor or client. Close attention to how the client responds to a paraphrase provides clues as to its appropriateness. They may be so obvious as to indicate that the offering does not seem quite right, in which case it can be retracted immediately. Or the clues may be subtle, in which case one may want to check on the fit. Rogers checked a lot, querying: 'Have I got that right?', 'Does that seem like it . . . ?', 'Is it a bit like that?', and so on.

When engaged in *reflection*, we discriminate between the cognitive aspects of what the client is saying and the feelings that seem to go with the cognitions and make sure that, whatever else is included in the response, the feelings are addressed. The difference between the paraphrase and the reflection is thus one of degree rather than kind. The signs of the feelings may be either explicit or implicit. When focusing on some aspect of their lives, clients may talk openly about how they feel about it (e.g. 'I try to make him understand but I can't get through to him. It's so upsetting.'). Here the reflection might assume the form, 'Uh huh. As hard as you try to get through, somehow it just doesn't work, and it's distressing.' Alternatively, clients' feelings may be implicit in what they say, in which case counsellors may want to be slightly interpretive in expressing their sense of the feelings involved. For example, a client may say, 'I try and try and try to make him understand and no matter what I try nothing seems to work.' When making such a remark, the client looks and sounds in a particular way and, putting it all together, it may be a safe bet that a struggle is being addressed. It is also possible that negative feelings of various sorts are associated with the struggle, such as frustration or perhaps even anger. All of these possibilities have to do with the zone of feelings accompanying the client's response and make available to the counsellor a range of responses. A safe response, but one that nevertheless touches upon feeling, might be, 'You've been trying to get through to him, and it's been a real struggle.' A somewhat riskier response is, 'You've tried very hard to get through to him, and I'm sensing that's it's been very frustrating for you.' Even riskier would be, 'You've been trying and trying to get through, without success, and I'm sensing that's making you feel really upset, perhaps even angry, inside.' Notice that the third response may do more to connect with the client's experience than the first, depending on its accuracy and on the client's readiness to receive it. On the other hand, if it is off target, then it will slow the client down more than would the first response (but even then, as indicated, we can always check with the client and regroup, and can bank on the client's tolerance in the process). It is the overall sense of the client's experience in the given moment that inclines us to choose one response over another.

This person-centred style of dialogue is illustrated in Box 4.2.

Box 4.2
Illustration of the person-centred style

Counsellor	So, it's a mixed world.
Client	Yeah, I don't know what things are bothering me. But I don't know [pause] I guess I can't [pause] I [pause] I don't know.
Counsellor	You haven't been able to connect it with anything, sort of. **[paraphrase]**
Client	It drives me nuts.
Counsellor	It's hard to talk about. **[reflection]**
Client	I felt like crying at first, but nothing would (long pause).
Counsellor	Ever since the bird died, or [pause]? [a reference to an earlier session; **bid for clarification**]
Client	Yeah. But it's not [pause] like I can connect that.
Counsellor	So it's not. You don't think that it's connected with that, particularly? **[paraphrase embedded in a closed question]**
Client	Yeah. Like especially today (pause). I keep wondering if it's connected to self-pity.
Counsellor	So you sort of doubt yourself? **[reflection]** So at the same time you feel bad but also saying to yourself, 'I shouldn't be feeling bad'. **[reflection]** You're fighting yourself all the time. **[reflection]**

This example is drawn from the therapy session experienced by the client mentioned in Chapter 2 who had had difficulty with her 'why?' question (see Box 2.1). Immediately following this counselling session, as part of a research enquiry, the client brought to me an audiotape of it. We replayed it together, with her stopping the replay at points of interest or significance. Part of her commentary on the above segment of the interaction with the counsellor reported in Box 4.2 is given in Box 4.3. These comments nicely confirm the usefulness of the person-centred way of being, infused as it is into what I have been referring to as the person-centred style of communicating. As indicated earlier, not every client reacts so favourably to this way of being and communicating. Those who react negatively to it appear to be in the minority, however, at least in terms of what I have found in my enquiry into the client's experience of counselling. Furthermore, even they appreciate it at certain junctures in their counselling sessions. Thus, being this way with clients is generally experienced favourably, apart from any theoretical and empirical justification for it. Hence, it is an very useful style to learn.

Box 4.3
The client's comment on the segment of the counselling session

Client OK, uh, what's she's been doing all this time is, uh, (pause) more or less prompting me to get it out and (pause) it's (pause) Like, there's times when you feel crazy, when you're telling people these things, right? But by her doing that it's (pause) it's like, uh, an assurance that she's (pause) she doesn't think that. Like, that she is understanding what you're (pause) what you're going through. Or maybe not even understanding, just that she's listening.
Researcher She's certainly trying to understand.
Client Yeah.
Researcher Yes.
Client So I just (pause) those, I think were, uh (pause) I wouldn't say that they're neutral because they do, uh, affect me. Like, if, if (pause) there was no response, if she sat back and didn't say anything, then I would probably have to stop and wonder where she was, where I was going with her.

Learning the style

Provided beginning counsellors are willing, the rudiments of the style may be learned very quickly. Trainees just have to decide on the one hand to refrain from asking too many closed questions, making interpretations early in the relationship with the client and from giving advice and, on the other, to try as much as possible to limit their responses to minimal encouragements, open-ended questions, bids for clarification, repetitions, paraphrases, reflections, and enquiries into the accuracy of their responses. Indeed, it has been demonstrated that a mere five minutes of instruction to this effect can result in a statistically significant increase in performance of the style (Quartaro and Rennie, 1983; Toukmanian, Capelle and Rennie, 1978). All counsellor trainees have the ingredients of the style prior to training and so, when given the explicit instruction to downplay ways of conversing that are at variance with it and of enhancing others that implement it, trainees discriminate among these various impulses and act accordingly, if willing.

Many beginning counsellors have difficulty actually using the style because it seems strange, however. This feeling of strangeness is understandable. After all, it *is* a bit weird to converse in this way. It is certainly not the way people engage in ordinary conversation, at least among adults (adults often talk with children in this way). Looked at superficially, it can seem almost comical; indeed, it has been the object of parodies by comedians like Mike Nichols and Elaine May, and of jokes. Correspondingly, especially when feeling that clients want us to solve their problems for them, it is easy to feel that they will laugh at us if we engage in this way carrying on a dialogue. Moreover, until this way of responding comes naturally, it feels wooden, robotic and mechanical – which, quite appropriately, trainees rebel against. In the early going, trying to communicate in terms of the style may seem false and it is difficult to believe that it does any good at all.

It helps to alter this impression if one is in the role of the client rather than the counsellor. Being on the receiving end can be very different than being a witness. This is because as clients we are interested in ourselves more than the other person and do not want that person to get in our way. Thus, what appears as a style from the outside perspective is not necessarily experienced that way at all when we are attending to ourselves. Instead, it is a presence that is very much in the background yet has the effect of slowing us down, moving us further into our experience of ourselves and sharpening it. The disclosures of the above research participant indicate that she was more sensitive to whether or not her counsellor was taking her seriously and was willing to listen to her than she was in getting some form of 'heavy duty' counselling. She was struggling to identify why she was feeling the way she was. This was her struggle; her locus of attention was within herself. In the language of counselling, she was processing her experience. She experienced her counsellor as a prompter of that processing. She did not expect the counsellor to initiate and control it. Indeed, clients may not only not expect such control, they may not want it. This was brought out vividly by another research participant who, being a person trained in counselling herself, actually described her experience in terms of the construct of processing (Box 4.4). (Note that even though in the excerpt this participant addressed 'Why?', she is not the participant in the earlier excerpts.)

Box 4.4
A counsellor's experience of counselling

'It's like, the big question is "Why?" But there is more than that, you know. Like, you cannot say everything that is functioning inside. It's like there's a lot – there's a process inside. That process needs to be fed. But not disturbed. And for me, putting too much energy into to explain [to] the other – if he [i.e. her therapist] wanted to understand too much, it would be bothering me and my process [pause] I mean, I listen to myself. It's not very interesting what I am *saying* [my emphasis]. What's important is what's happening inside of me.'

From 'Storytelling in psychotherapy: The client's subjective experience' (Rennie, 1994c)

Thus, when staying within the client's field of awareness, the counsellor usually has a much more powerful effect than would seem to be the case from the vantage point of external observation. When counsellors in training begin to realize this, adoption of the style becomes easier.

Summary

Although not unaware of the counsellor by any means, clients come to counselling with the intention to focus on themselves; indeed, the institution of counselling gives them permission to do so. In their self-focus, they engage paths to meaning. This engagement is inward, with clients' awareness of the counsellor becoming remote unless the latter does something to force attention away from themselves. Person-centred and experiential counsellors know both the importance to clients of their searches for meaning and how active they are in these quests. The quests are tinged with felt-senses, which also guide the progress along the paths. Correspondingly, we as counsellors do what we can to enhance clients' quests by working with the edges of their experiences while staying as much as possible in the background, out of the way. This way of being is facilitated if we engage in what I have referred to as the person-centred style.

This way of being and communicating with clients may seem from an external perspective to be rather passive but, in fact, it is very active and involves a great deal of work. We are listening intently to what the client is saying and trying to understand it, actively comparing it in our minds to what has been said before, trying to get a sense of the edge of the client's felt-sense. Also, while doing this, we have our own thoughts, feelings, memories of our own experiences, anticipations and theoretical formulations (if they arise in us). We do not encourage such internal activity; indeed, we want to shut it out as much as possible in order to experience clients as they experience themselves. However, it is impossible to shut out our internal happenings entirely. They just happen. This is another reason why we prefer the style. It provides a linguistic structure that helps to prevent us from giving voice to our internal happenings, from focusing attention on ourselves.

This way of putting it seems to me to sum up what is involved in the person-centred style and the reason for it, especially within this literalist perspective. Yet, interestingly, within this summary are the seeds of something that is integral to the experience of being a person-centred counsellor and which greatly enriches the whole picture. I am referring to our experience of ourselves as we interact with clients. In broad terms, this aspect bears upon the matter of the counsellor's congruence. As indicated, Rogers himself increasingly emphasized the importance of congruence as he got older but, apart from indicating that he increasingly felt comfortable in expressing where he was at congruently in being transparent (Bozarth, 1990b; also see Van Belle, 1980), he never said much about how he worked with his own experience while counselling. Alternatively, succeeding generations of person-centred counsellors (e.g. Lietaer, Mearns, Thorne) have stressed congruence and have also begun to address what authentically being themselves from moment-to-moment in counselling entails and how it enters into the process of counselling. This is very much my interest as well, and is focused on in the next chapter, when I address how the counsellor's expression of inner experience through the use of figurative language may enhance empathic contact with the client.

5
Vivid Language: Liberating the Secondary Stream of Consciousness

Our minds are very busy when we listen to clients. We attend to what they are saying and to how they are saying it, as well as to their body language. Meanwhile, we undergo any number of reactions: we have feelings, memories, associations, fantasies, anticipations, theoretical knowledge, visual images and metaphors arising in us. In one sense, it seems extraordinary that these happenings can occur when we are actively attending to the client. Yet we cannot become our clients, we can only understand them by living within our own experience of them. However, looking at the counsellor's relationship with the client in this way is troubling if we want to believe that it is possible to be outside ourselves and totally in the world of the other and thus objective in this sense. In the atmosphere of such mistrust of our inner experience, it is easy to dismiss it – or, at least, not to express it.

We preclude potentially useful discourse when dismissing our inner reactions in response to any such fear that they are going to get in the way of the client's experience. There is a growing body of opinion in the person-centred community, shared with existential counsellors and interpersonal counsellors, that such reactions may indeed relate meaningfully and even deeply to the client's experience. It is also increasingly recognized that, when we disclose internal reactions that relate meaningfully to the client's experience, it is greatly valued by clients. It allows them to get to know us a little as persons and allows them to feel more equal to us.

Our internal reactions as we counsel clients are basically of three types. They have to do with the client's path to meaning, with our relationship with the client, or that with ourselves. Only the first two have right of entry into the counselling discourse, while the third is best separated from the other two and kept to ourselves. I address in Chapter 6 the significance and role that may be played by subjective reactions about the relationship with the client. In this chapter I attend to reactions that seem to have to do with our sense of the client's experience.

Among the many types of such reactions, visual images and

metaphors are especially likely to be connected in some way with the client's path to meaning. When we have other kinds of reactions like recollections, associations, categorizations or theorizations, even though they may be related meaningfully to the client's experience, they may nevertheless shift the path somewhat if offered. Images and metaphors, on the other hand, often arise in us when we are intensely trying to follow the path. Two processes seem to be involved. The first is a visualization of the scenes in a story narrated by the client. As the client uses language to re-create a given event, we both take up the story linguistically and visualize it as we go along. I shall call this kind of visualization 'concrete'. The second is symbolization. In this case, what the client is saying is complex. In such a moment either a verbal metaphor or a visual image which is also a metaphor may come to us that seems to capture the central meaning of what is being said. In this case, then, when visualization is involved, it is symbolic.

Even though both concrete and symbolic visual images and metaphors are especially likely to be connected to the client's experience in some way, they may also arise as intrusions of our personal experience that is catalysed by something that the client has said. The client has 'hit a nerve' in us. This is not to say that even such personal experience may not be connectable in some way with the client's experience (although it may not). But even if it is, the connection may be remote from the immediacy of the path.

Appropriate use of images and metaphors arising in us thus requires appraisal. We need to detach momentarily from attending to the client in order to get a sense of whether they have to do with our experience of the client's experience or with our experience of ourselves independent of the client. I do not wish to minimize the subtleties involved in the attempt to make this discrimination. Even when being alert to the possibility that we may be projecting our own experience and after trying to catch ourselves doing it, it is possible to make mistakes. But nor do I think that this possibility should prevent us from making the attempt to discriminate in the interest of using these kinds of inner experience. After all, we can always enquire about any reactions given by a client indicating a lack of fit. Indeed, we can enquire in any case, although we would want to be careful here because such enquiry breaks into the client's flow. Whenever finding that our offering does not fit, we quickly discard it and invite the client to get back on track. Alternatively, if the presentation does fit, it may enhance the client's experiencing in a way that exceeds what would have occurred if we had taken the safer route of staying tightly within the literalness of their language.

I shall address concrete visual images, and symbolic images and metaphors in turn.

The concrete visual image

As indicated, among the images that we experience while listening to clients are visualizations of the scenery of an event being described by clients. As they describe having undergone a given experience, and especially if it was an event of some sort that is characterized in the form of a story, we may imagine them undergoing the experience.

Example

Let us say a client had a psychologically abusive mother against whom he could never win so that he learned to be compliant, never expressing his hurt (I am thinking of someone whom I counselled in the past). He describes this, indicating how as a child he was well-mannered and never fought back. He reveals how it got so bad by the time he was ten years old that he would huddle on the staircase in the house, hugging his knees and burying his head in them. He narrates how he would stay like that for two hours at a time, not moving and impervious to entreaties to come out of it.

When he depicts this scene, we are likely to see him as he was then, as we hear his account. The fact that our experience is twofold means that we have a choice between responding in terms of the client's language or in terms of what we saw as we listened to him. Should we search for the edge of his experience as expressed linguistically, we may respond in ways such as, 'The only way you could find peace was to separate yourself that way.' Or 'You had to go to that extreme in order to feel safe.' Alternatively, we may describe what we see. Here we may say something like, 'You know, I see you so clearly. You're so small. You're tightening yourself into the smallest ball possible, almost as if to make yourself disappear. You're gripping your knees so hard your hands are drained of blood. You're trembling but trying to hide it. You're secretly crying, and trying to hide that too.'

Notice the difference between the two responses. The reflection of the client's language is on track and would probably stimulate further thoughts and feelings about the event. The expression of the image has more of a gut-wrenching quality to it. It may stimulate the client to relive more fully the experience, as opposed to partly reliving it and partly talking about it, as he may do in response to the first type of intervention.

To express imagery in this way is to implement what Rice (1974) has referred to as an *evocative* reflection. She found that the recollection of the actual scenery involved in an emotional event helps the client to re-experience the sensations experienced during the event and, correspondingly, the emotions that went with them. In turn, heightening the client's emotional re-experiencing of the event stimulates a flood of images and associations that pave the way toward coming to terms with the event. Let us look at this more closely.

The utilization of imagery in this way usually has the effect of heightening clients' recall of an event. It halts their 'horizontal' flow within their track and stimulates a 'vertical' descent into an aspect of the track. In the case of my client, then, the descent included the emotional pain associated with his quest to understand himself by way of remembering his relationship with his mother. It is important to point out, however, that going 'vertical' like this is recommended only if it is considered more useful than allowing clients to stay in the horizontal flow. After all, we may have the sense that, even though what they are focusing on is important, they seem headed toward something more important.

Rice maintains that the use of visualization is especially appropriate when the client is experiencing a *problematic reaction point* (Rice and Saperia, 1984). By this term they mean a problematic reaction of some sort that occurred at a particular point in time. In this moment, the client reports having experienced an emotional reaction to an event that was out of keeping with what the situation called for. For example, when describing an event the client may say, 'I don't know what came over me. It was such a silly little thing that happened, yet I felt completely devastated.' Rice and Saperia contend that when this sort of disclosure is made it means that the client has temporarily lost the ability to evaluate accurately the deeper significance of the event with the result that its impact remains. This is where the counsellor's drawing upon imagery to stimulate the client to reconstruct the scenery of the event is useful because it helps the client to recapture what was felt at the time and the various contributions to the feeling. Correspondingly, this unfolding of the contributions to the problematic reaction helps the client to reconceptualize it and work through it.

There is speculation that the connection between imagery and feelings may have something to do with the encoding of experience. It is thought that emotional experience may be more directly connected to sensory images than to language (Bucci, 1985; Paivio, 1986). In this view, referential processing (Bucci, 1985), or linguistic representation of sensory images, recovers emotion more effectively than does the use of language to address experience already encoded linguistically. Thus, it may be for this reason that the recruitment of sensory images seems to deepen the emotional re-experiencing of an event, in turn leading the person closer to the root of those feelings.

Symbolic visual images and metaphor

When engaged with clients, we listen with a keen ear for the meaning of what they are saying. This activity is not easy at times. We may be presented with a surfeit of concrete details with few clues as to what they mean to the client. Moreover, what is being said now may only make sense in terms of what was said before, perhaps sessions ago. Occasionally, as we are actively engaged in this way, either an image or a verbal metaphor spontaneously comes to us that seems to capture the essence of what the client is experiencing in the moment.

Example

To illustrate, let us go back to the client recalling huddling on the stairs. As he talks, we may have an image of a pupa in a cocoon. At first the image seems bizarre: 'Yikes! Where did *that* come from?', we may wonder. Indeed, its bizarreness will make us want to consider it to try to get a sense of whether, perhaps, it is some sort of eruption of our own unconscious issues. In this case, while doing this, we may realize that there is in fact something about the image that fits the client incredibly well. First, it symbolizes the self-protection that is very much the feeling-tone of the client's experience as he engaged in his recollection. Furthermore, as part of the self-protection, there is an element of hiddenness, because the pupa is hidden inside the cocoon.

This much may come to us in a flash. Meanwhile, the client is still talking. While doing our best to stay with him, we may work further with the image and realize that there is still more to it. Connected with the pupa in an earlier metamorphosis is a caterpillar, a worm, which is very much how the client felt as a child. In addition, the theme of metamorphosis is coincident with that of transformation, and here we encounter an example of how a symbolic image like this may pertain to more than one meaning context (cf. Angus and Rennie, 1988, 1989). Even though the client has not addressed it in his account of being huddled on the stairs, we remember that on other occasions he has mentioned that when a child he often wished he were someone else. We further remember that, when he was twelve, he experienced a dramatic change of personality: he became filled with hate, a desire for revenge and, above all, wanted to be free. The symbol of the pupa undergoing metamorphosis captures all of these elements. Nor does it end there, we discover. The symbol of the cocoon also has to do with something akin to hibernating, being asleep. Although it was not a part of his recollection of huddling on the stairs, on other occasions he has revealed that for years he has been sleeping a lot as a means of escape.

Notice the amount of what Freud referred to as 'condensation' involved in the image. It is packed with meaning; it is very much like a dream image. For this reason I have to think that, when they arise in us, they are coming out of our unconscious – certainly our preconscious. Even though we are not aware of it, we are working in this 'zone' of ourselves, trying to understand the client, and an image of this sort is the result.

Obviously, in the foregoing example, I fully exercised the image of the pupa in a cocoon. It is easy to do this speculatively, when away from the counselling situation. In the actual situation, we may do the same thing while doing our best to attend to the client, but very likely not to the same extent. This activity involves quickly alternating between letting go of the image in order to hear what the client is saying *now* and retrieving the image, during a brief moment when we feel it is safe, in order to let the meaning of the symbol come to us further. We may engage in several of these recursions, each taking only a split second or more, before deciding on its aptness and on whether or not to say anything about it even if it is apt. Alternatively, and perhaps even more likely, we may stop trying to sense its meaning after realizing only one or two of the connections, knowing that there are very likely to be other fits, other correspondences, because it *feels* profound.

When they fit, images of this type are not only symbolic but also metaphorical in the sense that they unite into one meaning two or more different meanings (see Angus and Rennie, 1989). As such they may be so rich as to capture many of the main features of clients' issues and adjustments. These may include deep, painful feelings that are difficult to think about. The power of such an image is a consideration that needs to be taken into account when deciding whether to share it, and how to do it if shared. Several options are open. One is not to share it at all. Interestingly, there is evidence that, even in this case, our dialogue is more empathically in tune with the client's experience, according to clients' reports (see Box 5.1). By the same token, should we decide to impart the image, several ways are open to us. The safest tactic is to present the image without any interpretation of its meaning, in which case we might say something like, 'It's almost as if you're in a cocoon.' Doing it this way, clients have the freedom to do with it as they wish. They may take the metaphor and run with it, much as I

> **Box 5.1**
> **The counsellor's imagery as an empathic lens**
>
> Shaul (1994) did an interesting study of the impact of a counsellor's image on the client's experience of empathy irrespective of whether or not the image was communicated to the client. Shaul arranged for therapists/counsellors to signal when, during a counselling session, they experienced an image. The session was audiotaped. Immediately after the session, he met with the counsellor and together they replayed the tape to locate such moments. Using the technique of Interpersonal Process Recall (IPR) (Kagan, 1975; for its application to counselling research, see Elliott, 1986; Rennie, 1995), Shaul interviewed the counsellor about his or her recalled experience of the moments immediately before, during and immediately following the image, regardless of whether or not it had been communicated to the client. The researcher then independently replayed the same tape footage to the client and did an IPR interview of his or her recalled experience of those moments with the counsellor. Shaul found that the clients experienced the counsellor as being more empathic after the counsellor had experienced the image regardless of whether the latter had communicated it. The investigator interpreted his findings as indicating that counsellor imagery acts as an empathic lens, even when it is not expressed.

have done in the example above. Alternatively, they may work with a single aspect, or element, using language such as: 'Hmm. Yeah. I'm hidden from the world.' Or, 'Yeah. I'm protected.' Or, 'Yeah, I'm the next thing to a worm.' Or, 'Hmm. Yes. It's like I'm becoming something else.' Taking up any of these alternatives involves an opening, a step as Gendlin puts it, and we are wise to stay close to their experience (with the kinds of empathic responses addressed in Chapter 4) as they explore it. While all this is going on, we are aware of how clients seem as we convey the image – whether it is enticing or, perhaps, threatening in some way. If unsure of just how they are reacting to it, we always have the option of enquiring, by saying something like, 'Hmm. Now that I've put it that way, I can't quite get how you're reacting to it. Does the idea of a cocoon work for you or . . . ?' With such an opening, clients are given a signal that they need not defer to us and they may feel freer to tell us that it is not working well, or perhaps that it is rather scary to think of it in this way. After all, because they are inclined to defer, clients may go ahead and work with the image by, say, focusing on one element of it, as described, but do so half-heartedly. It's important to be alert to the energy in the client's uptake.

If there is good energy, then the field is open to us to feel our way into the extent to which the client senses and is willing to work with some of the other elements. Again, depending on how clients seem in the moment and on our knowledge of how they have responded to similar initiatives in the past, we may want to proceed very slowly and carefully, or we may feel that we can safely be more actively co-constructive. In the first case, we put the ball in their court every time we explore the possibility of yet another edge, through the use of probes such as: 'Is there anything else that seems connected to it, anything else that comes up?' Or, 'Does that about capture it, or does there seem to be more there?' Or, 'Does that seem to capture the full sense of it?' We track whatever clients come up with in reply to such queries; this particularly includes their resistance, should they signal it by indicating that there is more there but that they don't want to get into it. On the other hand, and again influenced by our sense of our relationship with the client as well as of his/her relationship with the image in the moment, we may introduce one or more of the meanings that we attach to the symbol as yet another offering to the client. If done tentatively, then clients have room to deny the significance of the offering or to change it so that it works for them, and then carry on from there. Moreover, an offering in this way may stimulate them to catch yet another edge, resulting in an exciting trading back and forth of sensed edges of meaning – in a collaborative engagement with the image (see Angus and Rennie, 1988; Gendlin, 1996). An additional benefit of working in this way is that when the image is rich with meaning, it may be used in the future as a pithy expression encapsulating a complex theme (Angus and Rennie, 1989). Thus, in the case of our example, in a subsequent dialogue, all the client or counsellor would have to do would be to refer to 'the cocoon' in order for a flood of understanding to come into place.

Verbal metaphors

Other metaphors as signs are verbal. The number of possible such metaphors is legion. Examples are 'It seems like you're a pariah.' (i.e. You're feeling like an outcast, like an untouchable, like no one wants to have anything to do with you, like you're evil inside, like you should be locked away, etc.); and 'In that moment I was king.' (i.e. I was top of the power hierarchy, people looked up to me, I didn't have to compete any more, I had no money worries, I had satisfied all my desires, etc.). Such expressions are metaphorical when used figuratively rather than literally, and when the meaning-spaces of the terms envelop the individual to whom the term is being attributed. Moreover, like visual images, these meaning-spaces have fuzzy edges which accommodate the nuances of the meaning involved. There is room for subjectivity in the use of metaphors (Kiesler, 1996).

Many verbal metaphors originate in visual images that gradually are no longer 'seen' when the metaphor is used because it has become part of everyday language, such as clichés and slang. Thus we may say (in American English, at least), 'It sounds like you're at the end of your rope.' (i.e. You've tried everything, you're totally frustrated, you're completely exasperated, you can't do this anymore, you've had it, there's nothing left to do but give up, etc.); or 'You're a rock.' (i.e. You're steadfast, reliable, solid, immovable, committed, determined, unwavering, obdurate, not going to change your opinion, etc.). In fact, with clichés such as these, it is sometimes difficult to know what the original imagery may have been. What imagery first went with 'end of your rope', for example? As I first thought of this when choosing it as an example, I realized that I had always subconsciously thought it arose from the image of a noose around one's neck. On further consideration, however, that image does not necessarily fit (except in the sense of 'there's nothing left but to hang myself'); the image of being on a tether and able to go no further may be more appropriate. The point is, I did not need the image to know what the term means, because it has become part of my language.

It would be natural to think that clichés like these wouldn't do much to capture clients' experience in counselling. Instead, we may be inclined to think that only original metaphors – metaphors that 'organically' are produced during the course of our interaction with clients, like the 'cocoon' metaphor in the visual mode – would be useful. This does not appear to be the case, however. Angus and Rennie (1989) found that clients may represent very complex meanings with seemingly banal, clichéd metaphors. This finding is important because without it we may be inclined not to use clichés when they arise in us, or to undervalue their impact when we do use them (and the same can be applied to the significance we may attach to them when produced by clients). I ran into this with one of my clients (see Box 5.2) as I realized when a colleague interviewed him about the experience of being counselled by me (Box 5.3).

Box 5.2
The power of a casually offered cliché

A number of years ago I had a client ('Henry') who was a law student, having entered university about ten years after high school. In that decade he had developed various interests, which he did not want to sacrifice to a professional career path. Meanwhile, he was competitive and distressed about not getting the kind of grades that he wanted; although not in real trouble academically, failure seemed a possibility. Along with this was a worry that he was not as intelligent as many of his classmates; he seemed to have to work harder than many of them. All of this had led to a conflict about working at his studies. At times he resented the amount of work he had to do but generally he knuckled under because his fear of not doing well outweighed the desire to continue to live a balanced lifestyle. The worst of it was that even that amount of work didn't seem to be doing the trick. This was the framework of the particular session upon which I am focusing – one that we had scheduled for my research. The arrangement was that we would videotape the session, then a colleague would conduct an IPR (Kagan, 1975) type of enquiry into Henry's recollection of the counselling session. For about half of the session, Henry and I had been exploring his concerns. Meanwhile, I had been trying to get a sense of where he was at. It was in this context that the following exchange occurred.

Client   My feeling would be that I can wipe As right off the bat. There's only a chance of, you know – the best chance is a B. If I had a B I'd say, 'Well, I have to go in a sort of holding pattern, with some fine tuning'. If I got a C, the new pattern would not be dissimilar to the present pattern, but more major tinkering around the Bs. If I got Ds or Fs, that would really be [pause].

Counsellor   That would be tough to take because I'm sensing that you're not sure that you've got sufficient reserve left or sufficient flexibility (*Client:* Yeah) to come up with a strategy that [pause].

Client   Exactly. That, that hit it on the head because that thing about 'reserve' so often, uh, I'm not really flaked out yet compared with, with, I don't know, late February as an undergrad. I, uh, you, I sometimes wonder if I can drag myself out of bed but, because I recognize that progression of the disease [he meant his difficulties] so, so readily now, so often I have said to myself, 'I know I don't have that reserve.' If I get to that point again I just won't be able to reproduce that effort again regardless of desire . . . I just don't think I've got that push anymore.

> *Box 5.3*
> **The client's commentary on the exchange in Box 5.2**
>
> Client   I was sort of surprised at that [i.e. the 'reserve' remark] because, uh [pause]
> Researcher   Surprised at what?
> Client   At, at Dave, at the acuity of David's response because I was thinking, in that section of the tape [i.e. of the counselling session], 'I know I have given to David very many things. I have used words like "inferiority complex" so, you know, even though he's a psychologist, he just doesn't have to be too smart to, to say to me "inferiority complex".' But I, I couldn't dredge up in my memory anywhere where I had said that question of *reserve* to him. And the way it came out, because I was sort of trying to get to that. Even though I'm aware within myself that this is something that I've been feeling recently – this question of no reserve – I wasn't at that point in time thinking of that term. I know that I was groping toward it because it was not a familiar feeling . . . I can't see where I was saying that but when he said it, it *really* met it. Because I can't tell you much that, that whole joining together of all those feelings of what it was like back in undergrad and my (pause) the stirring of the same feeling.

When I heard the tape of the research interview with this client, I was stunned. Although I recalled having the feeling that 'insufficient reserve' tied together a lot of what he had said, I had no idea that it had made such an impact. It had seemed to me to be more in keeping with an ordinary reflection rather than a metaphor as such. It was only later, after learning of his commentary on its effect on him, that I realized that it indeed had been a metaphor that had powerfully connected together the various strands of his experience extending back over several weeks, even months.

Even though Henry had given a strong 'Exactly' and had elaborated on 'insufficient reserve' after I had made the remark, I hadn't given his endorsement and all that went with it the attention it deserved. Instead, I had gone on to a new topic – the strategies he might use depending on what his grades proved to be. Henry's commentary revealed that I had made a mistake.

The need for sensitivity

As in any kind of responding to clients, mistakes can be made when we operate within our own agendas and we lose touch with where they are at in the moment. I had fallen into this after the 'insufficient reserve' offering to Henry. Why? First, I had felt deeply his need to get a handle on his problem. But there had been something else as well. I had been thrown by his indication that he had already applied the metaphor to himself. It wasn't new to him and I think I assumed that because he had already gone over it in his mind, obviously it had not worked, which justified going on another tack. In fact, as came out in his commentary, Henry had indeed applied the term 'insufficient reserve' to himself but, during the week prior to the counselling session in question, *he had forgotten it and was groping for it in the counselling session.* He had not mentioned that he had forgotten it, and so I had simply assumed that he had remembered it. This was why it had hit him like a ton of bricks. He had been astonished that I had somehow seen him so clearly. He reported further on in the research enquiry that, while engaging in discourse with me after that point, he had been trying to remember if he had ever mentioned the metaphor in earlier meetings with me. He had finally concluded that he had not done so. This section of his commentary to the research interviewer is very interesting, and important (Box 5.4). What it seems to tell us is that, even though Henry had applied the same term to himself from time to time prior to the session, and even though he had been groping for it in the session, when *I* had come up with it, rather than feeling relieved that his earlier sense of himself had been correct (i.e. that he really *did* have insufficient reserve), he had needed from me evidence that I had 'facts' to substantiate my use of the term. He was trying to sort out where I 'was coming from'. Had I put together information that he had given me, or had I somehow come up with some sort of incredible intuition – a 'lucky shot', as he put it? My sense of his struggle here is that he was searching for confirmation. If I had simply read his mind, then he would be no further ahead. Alternatively, if I had been alert to the same kind of information about himself that he knew about himself, and had come to the same conclusion as he had, then that would confirm the correctness of his own assessment.

Several important things thus come out of this commentary, especially because much in it is supported by the accounts of other participants in the study. First, it has a resounding impact on

> **Box 5.4**
>
> **Further comment by Henry**
>
> **Client** He's been tapping my phone, or something like that. But more than that, because that was sort of what I was getting at without realizing myself that *was* what I was getting at.
>
> **Researcher** OK. Uh, now you come, you really let him know that he hit the nail on the head. [They listen to some more tape] OK, you're spelling out your 'reserve' a bit. I wonder what you imagine Dave is doing in that. What's he thinking. Kind of, what's he trying to do here?
>
> **Client** Uh, hmmm. My only feeling in that section is that, uh, David's hit the nail on the head. I'm still in a sense of shock. It seems unreal, so I wanted to test it out because it could be a lucky shot.
>
> **Researcher** You're kind of saying, 'Spell it out a bit?'
>
> **Client** Yeah. I'm trying to see whether he's [pause] whether that matches, and if it does match, where did I give him the clues in the past. Like, have I said to him something about, 'Remember when I was tired and couldn't get out of bed?' He's not so much giving me those clues, nor am I getting the feeling that, that the specifics I'm giving him are filling him in anymore. So, at this stage, I'm uncertain about whether at this stage he has a sort of raw feeling for me or whether there's a little more – whether that raw feeling is discrete.

the client when the counsellor comes up with a metaphor that matches exactly what the client has thought about himself but has since forgotten and is now groping for. (I think we may safely assume that the key is the groping, in which case the same point applies to groping for the right word, irrespective of whether or not it has been found in the past.) Second, the accuracy of the counsellor's response may not necessarily move the client more deeply into the experience, depending on the context of the response (in this case, the client was preoccupied with the *basis* for the accuracy). Third, part of the client's response to the counsellor's response may be not only *covert* but also more regnant than the response given in the client's discourse with the counsellor. Finally, and perhaps most important, when counsellors have an agenda in mind other than staying close to the client's experience in the moment (as was the case with me in this segment of the counselling session), they may miss subtle clues signalling the presence of this covert activity and may, therefore, miss a major part of the impact of their responses.

Another consideration is that, when expressing a metaphor, it should fit smoothly into the client's track. This means that it works best when it is conveyed in a word or two. Elaborate metaphors (or complex responses of any sort, for that matter) require clients to tear their attention away from themselves and they do this with reluctance. I learned this the hard way. When working with another client ('Peter'), who had also agreed to participate in my research, I was given an insight into just how disrupting it is for the client when the counsellor launches into a long-winded discourse of some sort which is disjunctive with his or her track. While he talked in the counselling session with me, I had had an image of a sea broken by a series of islands and it seemed to me that this image spoke to his experience. I had felt pretty convinced of this but, in order to make my point, I not only gave the image but also explained what it meant to me and hence what it might mean to him. In short, I gave an interpretation that had more to do with my depths than with his, as his commentary on it points out (Box 5.5).

Box 5.5
An instance of the counsellor destroying the client's focus

'It's not a conscious purpose because I'm really sensitive towards people, if I say something that someone takes the wrong way, I feel lousy about it for a long time. I overreact. And even if Dave is saying something that isn't right, I don't disagree because I know he's trying real hard and everything, and I don't want to make him feel bad [but] starting at the beginning, the analogy didn't work for me – the sea and the mountains. And then it sank in a bit more. And then, he's just starting now, but he's going to get really excited, or really take things over, in a bigger way than he's done in the whole session. . . . Right now he's going to go right over my head and blow me over the whole – it's an analogy, and it really shook me around. I couldn't focus on anything, and it really slowed things down at this point.'

It can seen from the commentary the extent to which this was a mistake. There are other revelations as well. Richly apparent is the strength of Peter's inclination to defer to me even though I was very off target; also of note is his forgiveness. Admittedly, he may have indicated forgiveness because he knew that I would learn about what he was saying; still, it is not out of keeping with what other clients have indicated in a less constraining situation.

Summary

Visual imagery and its close cousin, metaphor, are potent stimuli. Imagery may be either concrete or symbolic. Concrete imagery is a picturing of the scenes narrated by clients as we listen to their stories. When conveyed to them, it may deepen their experience of the feelings they underwent during the events being narrated. In a similar vein, when the feelings are judged by clients to be overreactions of some sort, then the use of imagery in this way may help them to tease out the reasons for such reactions. Symbolic images, almost like dream images, tend to condense in highly efficient ways many strands of meaning. Such images may be threatening to clients, or may be assimilable to varying extents. Sensitivity and tact are required when deciding whether or not to attempt to work with symbolic images, and, if so, how. In any case, there is evidence suggesting that the experience of such images empathically attunes the counsellor's responding subsequent to the experience of the image, whether it is communicated explicitly or not.

Verbal metaphors work best if they are pithy and apt so that they do not derail the client. Like symbolic images, apt metaphors recruit and integrate many strands of meaning. Both forms, if pertinent, thereafter enable the client and counsellor to refer to complex meaning in a word or two, thus economizing the communication between them.

Overall, the decision to use imagery and metaphor has to be made in the context of a judgement about what would seem to benefit the client from moment to moment. Clients who are introspecting well and close to their feelings may find counsellor-imparted imagery more disruptive than helpful, while clients who are having difficulty getting in touch with their feelings may be aided by imagery. And clients who are anxious because they are burdened with many tendrils of poorly defined thoughts and feelings may experience a joyous feeling of integration and relief when presented with an apt symbolic image or metaphor.

Our imagery and metaphors are disconcerting because there is always the possibility that they have more to do with us than with the client. They require appraisal in the interest of sorting out their fit with the client's experience, and even after that it is difficult to be sure of one's judgement. These aspects make us hesitant to impart them. We can reduce our fears in this regard, however, when we realize that we can always check with the client on the pertinence of the offering. Moreover, we may be comforted by the fact that, even if we make a mistake, chances are it will not be a disaster. Clients generally handle our mistakes more robustly and tolerantly than we would expect, giving us a margin of safety.

When using imagery and metaphor, we break out of the tight constraints of being safe (and often banal) counsellors and become more interesting, stimulating, fresh, evocative and powerful. The potential rewards outweigh the risks. Hence, my suggestion is that we should pay attention to imagery when we experience it. If it seems to fit the client's experience and if the client may benefit from it, then we should trust it.

It is easier to feel comfortable communicating with clients in these ways once we have learned about metacommunication (see Chapter 8). I feel that other matters need to be attended to first before I am ready to address that way of being with clients, however. Our next consideration on our way to the discussion of metacommunication is the subject of transparency, or expressed congruence.

6
Transparency in the Relationship with the Client

I have suggested in earlier chapters that attention to the client's experience is more powerful than we may think and have given an understanding of why this is so. I have also taken the position that therapeutic power may be enhanced by stimulating the re-experiencing of emotion through the impartation of concrete imagery, and by using symbolic images and metaphor to condense and symbolize multiple themes. I have emphasized the importance of checking within ourselves the seeming accuracy of our sense of the client's experience as represented by the image or metaphor, and of checking with clients about their sense of its accuracy. At the same time, I have supported the venture by pointing out that we may feel reassured by evidence suggesting that, even if offerings of this sort are misplaced, clients usually tolerate disruptions in counselling so long as they are satisfied that, on the whole, the engagement with the counsellor is helpful.

The focus of the last chapter was clients' relationships with themselves. We feel free to maintain this focus when they actively pursue the meaning of felt-experience and we sense that their relationship with us is satisfactory. In this circumstance, clients expect little from us and welcome whatever facilitation we may provide. In turn, although we have to be vigilant when dealing with the appropriateness of an internal reaction, within that vigilance we can be open with our clients because we are congruent in our sense of what both we and our clients are doing.

It can happen that our experience of being a counsellor is not so straightforward and pleasant, however. There are times when we may be incongruent. We may be split between the image of ourselves that we try to convey to our clients and the image that we are secretly harbouring, between what we are doing with a client and the faith that we have in the approach, or between what we would like to believe about a client and what we really believe. Often disjunctions like these can be worked through, especially when there are grounds for believing that, overall, the client seems to be getting something out of our counselling. It is when we are sensing that the counselling is not going well that we may not be able to ignore them.

Incongruencies pertaining to our relationship with the client are basically of two types: self-depreciation and depreciation of the client. In the first case, we may find ourselves thinking thoughts like, 'I don't know what I'm doing' (when I should know), 'I can't help this person' (when I should be able to), 'I feel like a robot dishing out of this person-centred stuff' (when I should feel natural), 'I haven't a clue about what I should say' (when I should know exactly what to say), or 'I feel so upset right now I could cry' (when I should be able to maintain my composure). That I am suggesting we may also experience the second type of incongruency may seem surprising in view of what I have said about adopting a neutral attitude of concerned interest about clients. I stay with that admonition but now admit that it is aspirational. Despite the aspiration, we may at times have negative reactions about clients. We may find ourselves thinking, 'Golly. All he does is talk endlessly. I'm getting buried. I can't keep anything straight. I can't even listen to him any more: I'm too irritated.' Or, 'This woman is wearing me down. She's so dependent and draining; I know I'm withdrawing from her but I've got to; otherwise there'll be nothing left of me.' Or, 'I'm having trouble listening to him because he's so cavalier about what should be serious things; either he's conning me of he's lost touch with his feelings; why should I place myself in the position of throwing good money after bad?'

Coming off the high horse

Let us look first at self-depreciatory thoughts. These are not easily shared with clients. Particularly when we are learning to become counsellors, we are inclined to believe that we should look competent – experts at our craft. We are afraid that if we destroy this image our clients will lose faith in us and drop out of counselling. Moreover, it is difficult not to feel that we would be a failure should the client discontinue. Consequently, we may be inclined to suppress our sense of inadequacy, to sweep it under the rug. Even if we resist this temptation, it is still difficult to share it with our clients. Either way, they are not told of what we are going through. There is an irony involved in not disclosing our doubts about ourselves, however: even though we attempt to hide them, our clients are often aware of them anyway. They may be just as accomplished at 'reading' us as we are at reading them. If we are secretly quaking in our boots but attempt to assume a serene front of control and competence, the quaking is going to be conveyed by our conduct and manner (see also Braaten, 1986).

Clients' capacities to see through our screens, combined with their deference to us, make hiding a sense of inadequacy a very complicated affair. We do not feel good about ourselves and the client knows this, yet no one says anything. In addition, if clients are influenced to be unhappy with us because we're unhappy with ourselves, we do not hear of their unhappiness. Thus both counsellor and client may privately feel that the counselling is not working well, that it takes an effort to go to meetings and that it would be nice if the whole thing were ended; yet, because of the inhibitions jointly involved, the pretence is upheld that the counselling is going well. Unfortunately, the pretence may lead the counselling to continue for weeks, even months.

There is something that is very difficult for beginning counsellors to believe but which I have seen confirmed many more times than not: when we override our inhibition and disclose our felt-sense of weakness, the fact that we can openly admit it often increases rather than decreases the client's respect for us. What are the dynamics of this seeming paradox? As indicated, clients generally sense the incongruence that we are trying to hide. Thus, they sense something that we do not think they sense. Should we then elect not to reveal ourselves, our silence may be taken as an indication that our shakiness is more than we can handle. This sense not only gives grounds for clients' sense that we lack courage, it undermines their faith and trust in us (i.e. it creates the same negativities in the client that we fear will arise if we disclose our concerns). Alternatively, should we be open about our incongruence, it means to clients that we have separated ourselves from the disjunction and correspondingly may be superior to it. Thus, not only are clients in a position to ascribe courage to us, more fundamentally they may be reassured that, in our ability to talk about our felt-sense of inadequacy, we are rising above it. Moreover, there is good reason for clients to feel that our disclosure is promising. Typically, if we can bring ourselves to admit that we are harbouring feelings of inadequacy, the act of admitting them does a great deal to dispel them. It is very similar to stage fright. When paralysed with fear as we stand before an audience, admission of the fear breaks the tension and we can carry on.

This breaking of tension comes from another source as well: our performance anxiety arises in part from a belief that clients expect us always to know what we are doing and to never make mistakes. When we admit that we do not know everything, and when clients accept our admission as is so often the case, then we can let go of the preoccupation with our sense of inadequacy and draw upon the rest of ourselves, finding some strength. In short, we are as empowered by clients' acceptance of us as they are by our acceptance of them.

I am not suggesting that disclosure of such feelings should be done as a matter of course. It becomes pertinent when we are so upset that we are finding it difficult to function and there is a real danger that we are losing the client, in spirit if not in body. Short of that, we may well be hesitant about disclosing such concerns because doing so will shift the focus away from the client and onto ourselves, and we may thus want to get the focus back on the client as soon as possible. Nevertheless, if we decide to shift, it is best to be thorough; otherwise we may undermine the full therapeutic effect of the disclosure, both for us and for the client. For example, I may feel anxious about my ability to help a client, not only because I believe that I lack certain skills (the main source of my anxiety, let's say), but also because I sense that (a) the client is extremely upset; (b) that in being upset, she has difficulty making much sense of her experience; (c) that she has no support network and therefore is turning to me as a final resort; and that (d) in all of this, I very much want to help but am momentarily at a loss in terms of knowing what to do.

It is likely that if I said all of this, at the end of it I would feel totally exposed. However, if it is my sense that the counselling has reached a crisis point, such transparency may be precisely what is required. There is something rather wonderful about honesty as long as it is not used hurtfully. Notice that this particular disclosure has not only to do with me, but with the client as well, and this brings her back into the picture. The disclosure enables her to know that I have a strong sense of what she is going through. Although she may feel disappointed that I have no magic answer for it, she may also feel reassured by my declaration that her difficulty is not easy to solve. This is because my expression of my being stuck may confirm her own sense of being stuck and thus confirm that her judgement is sound. Moreover, she may feel that I am not going to give up on her. An ancillary effect of the full disclosure is that it may also allow her to experience me as a human being, as having 'come off my high horse'.

Hence, when disclosing an incongruence in the context of a crisis in counselling, it generally works best if we hold nothing back so long as we do not intend to be hurtful and are sensitive to what may be experienced as hurtful. Managing this entails reflexivity as we gather together and appraise the strands of our experience. This takes time and it pays not to rush, either when contemplating the incongruence or communicating it. A disclosure of this sort is best looked upon as a deliberate interruption of the tracking of the client's flow of experience because a more serious matter is at stake than the flow. Looking at it this way makes room for the disclosure.

Negative reactions to the client: dealing with the obvious

Try as we might to fight the feeling, at times we may find ourselves reacting negatively to clients. We may be afraid for them, afraid of them or irritated by them. As discussed above, we often have feelings like this in low intensities and they do not interfere with our functioning as counsellors. We manage to relegate them to the corner of our awareness. There are other times when negative feelings about the client constitute a major disjunction in our experience. Typically, the disjunction is greatest when it is connected with frustration about the client's progress. This disjunction may be intricate. We would like to believe that the aspect of the client that is contributing to our negative reaction is the same trait that interferes with the progress. Yet, it is easy to worry that our judgement is wrong and that what we are dealing with has more to do with us than the client – that it may be counter-transferential, to use the language of psychoanalysis. Should we doubt the reason for the negative reaction in this way, we may be inclined to quash it.

A tendency to self-blame when experiencing a negative reaction to a client is most common at the outset of our careers. When starting out we are insecure and are inclined to mistrust our judgement. We tend to fail to allow that the way we are feeling about the client is probably the way that everyone feels, because that is the way the client is. This is what I call failing to deal with the obvious. For example, let us say that I am working with an intelligent woman who has been in counselling with a number of counsellors for many years. She is an expert on counselling – and counsellors. I feel like I'm walking on egg shells whenever we meet. If I become active and animated, she subtly lets me know that I am overwhelming her; if I reflect, she seems to accuse me of being superficial. The main feeling that I have is that I am on trial and am not living up to her expectations.

I do not like this feeling. Dealing with it is not easy, however, because underneath it is a deeper feeling, the very kind of feeling that she seems to be accusing me of having: I'm not sure that I am giving her my best. There's a twinge of guilt there and it makes it difficult to confront her. I'm caught. Yet something has to be done, it would seem, because we're becoming more distant with each other; the counselling is moving towards if not entering crisis.

Now, if I were merely to draw her attention to her way of putting me on edge – walking on egg shells – that would be a confrontation. Doing that would be relatively easy because I could keep my other feelings out of it. The chances are, however, that she would experience it as an attack and become defensive. A more productive route is to begin by owning my own experience, including my concern that I might not be giving her my all, and by following the disclosure with a gently put and tentative conjecture about how my experience of myself may be connected in some way with what she is doing.

When doing all this, I try to leave no feeling unattended, getting in touch with what I have felt in the past and feel now. I reveal that I have felt very warm and close to her at times but that these feelings have been tinged with precariousness. I disclose that it seems to have been connected with a sense that she is always evaluating me and that I sometimes come up 'below standard', that I am often left with the feeling that I somehow always have to please her. I go on to explain that I often do not feel sure of my ground with her and cannot sort out whether I really am not functioning well or am being criticized unjustly. I conclude that regardless of the dynamics involved I have found myself being edgy when I have been with her of late and that I haven't looked forward to our meetings as much as before. I admit that I have felt myself withdrawing from her to a certain extent.

This is heavy-duty material but I find that its disclosure may be required in an effort to save a counselling relationship that has gone sour. What often happens is that the client responds that the way I feel is the same as the way everybody reports having felt with her. It is why she currently has no partner and why she despairs of ever finding another – she's too fussy and expects too much from people. When this kind of disclosure is given by the client, it puts the counselling on a whole new footing because it means that we can now use the relationship as a laboratory in which we can study her relationships with people in general.

When reading this, you may be reacting with discomfort. You may be wondering if you ever could or should be so candid about what you are feeling. You may be thinking that what I have described could be said about any relationship that has run into difficulty and you may be taken aback because earlier I led you to believe that there is something special about a counselling relationship that goes beyond ordinary ones. You may want to accuse me of being inconsistent, even hypocritical. The difficulty is that counselling is so complicated that it encompasses all that I have addressed thus far, and much more. It can be an other-centred form of communication in which the client is the focus and in which the counsellor can keep personal involvement at a low level. As Mearns and Thorne (1988) point out, it can also be an intense, gut-wrenching encounter at the deepest personal level wherein we feel as exposed as we would hope our clients would feel (more on encounter in the section on interpersonal psychotherapy below).

It all depends on what is happening. As I have said before, if the client is psychologically-minded and a hard worker, then a self-disclosing confrontation may never be required. Alternatively, if the counselling never seems to get off the ground or seems to get bogged down, or the client starts to cancel appointments, or calls in the middle of the night, or never starts serious work until ten minutes before the end of the counselling hour, or persists in challenging us about what we are doing, then we may feel so disturbed that we can no longer function properly. It is then that a crisis ensues and we are faced with a difficult choice: either we sweep it under the rug and try to carry on as if the disjunction does not exist or we attempt to deal with it directly.

I prefer the second option because it cuts through disjunctions on both sides. As illustrated above, in most cases the counsellor's disjunction is not strictly of his or her own making. Instead it is integral to and embedded in the relationship; the client is contributing to it as much if not more than the counsellor. Because clients are reluctant to speak up, it is up to the counsellor to make the first move. When the move is taken, a breath of fresh air blows through the relationship. Both make real contact; the counselling has a new quality because the client's way of being is identified, accepted and converted from a tacit disrupter of the counselling into the main object of interest in it. The obvious is being addressed and the crisis in the counselling relationship is addressed with it.

Comparison with interpersonal psychotherapy

The discerning reader will have noticed some similarities between the transparency addressed in this chapter and both contemporary interpersonal psychotherapy and object relations therapy as influenced by interpersonal therapy. There are also implications for the working alliance (cf. Bordin, 1979; Greenson, 1967; Sterba, 1934; Zetzel, 1956). When I suggest that addressing directly how we are feeling and behaving when in interaction with clients may amount to dealing with the obvious about the client, this is a loose way of describing what Kiesler (1982, 1996) has referred to as dealing with the (transferential) 'pulls' exerted upon us by clients. Moreover, when I allude to metacommunication and, indeed, devote an entire chapter to it later on in the book (Chapter 8), I am confirming the importance ascribed by interpersonal therapists to this mode of interaction. In closing this chapter, I shall discuss only the interpersonal aspect and reserve for the later chapter a comparison between metacommunication as used in the present approach versus the interpersonal psychotherapeutic application of it.

Interpersonal therapy is a technical approach based on the 'interpersonal circle', derived from Leary's (1957) original work. This theory and research is much too rich to summarize here. Moreover, there are several versions of how this theoretical work has been translated into therapeutic practice (for an excellent review of interpersonal theory and research, and of interpersonal psychotherapy, see Kiesler, 1996). Nevertheless, for our purposes, the main propositions characterizing interpersonal psychotherapy as seen in the light of Kiesler's (1996) review may be summarized as follows:

1 The interpersonal aspects of the client's being are more important than his or her intrapersonal aspects.
2 The client's relationship with the therapist/counsellor is typical of the client's relationship with everyone else.
3 In the broadest sense the relationship has to do with the two main dimensions of affiliation and dominance.
4 When relating interpersonally, clients 'pull' responses that are complementary to their own responses; thus, for example, submissive and hostile clients pull dominant and friendly responses respectively.
5 The client's way of relating interpersonally is habitual, entailing little if any self-awareness.
6 The counsellor's compliance with complementarity is important in order to establish the working alliance.
7 The pulls experienced by the counsellor may be either subjectively or objectively counter-transferential; it is likely that they are objectively so, but care must be taken by the counsellor to make an appropriate discrimination.

8 In order to effect change in the client, it is necessary for the therapist eventually to become asocial with the client; this asociality may entail aspects of one of the two main dimensions (acomplementarity) or of both of them (anticomplementarity).
9 The counsellor's asociality is confrontational to the client and must be conducted with care and sensitivity in order to maintain the working alliance.
10 Seemingly in keeping with the last point, the course of successful interpersonal therapy is characterized by complementarity in the early and late stages of therapy, with non-complementarity in between.

In the language of the present approach to counselling, interpersonal therapy (and especially as it is conceptualized and practised by Kiesler) places the client primarily in the role of patient and the therapist in that of agent. Although Kiesler sensitively acknowledges that it is always possible that the interpersonal therapist's counter-transferential responses are subjective, he holds that it is up to the therapist to sort out when this is the case and to respond to the client only in terms of what he refers to as objective counter-transferences. In taking this stance, Kiesler is thus adhering to objectivism characteristic of classical psychodynamic theory and inherited from the Cartesian-Lockean approach to epistemology (cf. May, 1958a; Rennie, 1997).

The difference between the theoretical framework of the present approach and that of interpersonal therapy has much to do with reflexivity. Once reflexivity as I have defined it is taken into account, then it is recognized that clients not only have relationships with themselves, they also experience their relationships with others in terms of their relationships with themselves, just as we have relationships with them in terms of our relationships with ourselves. The symmetry is thus complete except for the matter of balance between agency and patienthood in clients as opposed to ourselves. But even if it is granted that clients may be comparatively less agential than us, it is always possible that, in being a particular way with us, they are *not* in the grip of forces beyond their ken but instead are reacting realistically to the way we are. They may know this because they have checked their relationship with us against their relationship with others and have found that their reaction is not typical. Thus, they may decide that they are not being subjective (or 'transferential'), just as we might in virtue of our reflexivity come to the belief that we are not being subjective (or 'counter-transferential') in our interaction with a given client.

In the language of existential therapy (May, 1958b), the current approach recognizes that clients have a relationship with themselves (their *Eigenwelt* or 'own world') and experience the relationship with the counsellor (*Mitwelt* or social world) in terms of that first relationship. In contrast, contemporary interpersonal therapy downplays clients' *Eigenwelt* in favour of their *Mitwelt*. As such, the current approach is compatible not only with existential therapy but with feminist therapy as well. Nevertheless, how this difference plays out in the intensity of the counselling moment is subtle. As seen, in the present approach it is held to be important to pay attention to the source of internal reactions to the client and to try to ascertain whether they seem to be objective or subjective, just as Kiesler maintains. The difference is that in the present approach we are comparatively less confident that the discrimination can be made successfully. Instead, it is more readily assumed that it is possible that we have made a mistake, which constrains us to offer our reactions even more tentatively than interpersonal therapists offer their reactions. Correspondingly, there is an even greater readiness to negotiate, to pull back, to reconsider, or to dismiss the reaction, depending on how it is received by the client. The realization that we do not have cognitive privilege (i.e. the ability to perceive reality objectively as from the vantage point of a Titan or god; see Margolis, 1986; Rennie, 1998) increases our humility. Thus, the approach makes correspondingly greater room for what Buber and other existential therapists have referred to as *encounter* and, as such, is different than either literal person-centred therapy or the Kieslerian version of interpersonal therapy (see Van Belle [1980] for Buber's criticism that literal person-centred counselling precludes encounter).

Finally, recognition of clients' reflexivity creates a reluctance to rely primarily on technique, even if it has to do with the relationship with the client. Encounter transcends technique (May, 1958b). Instead, in the present approach, bringing the relationship into play entails determining the cogency of our reactions and, short of reversing roles, inviting clients to share their reactions to us, in the interest of establishing an encounter (more on this in Chapter 8, Metacommunication). In being an encounter, the results of such transactions have meaning not only for them but for ourselves as well. In the following chapter, I develop additional ways of assisting clients with their agency, by identifying and/or directing their processing of experience.

Summary

Transparency is the disclosure to the client of how we are experiencing ourselves in relation with the client and/or of how we are experiencing the client. When making a disclosure, the asymmetry of the counselling relationship is preserved in the important sense that we attempt to separate our personal, or 'countertransferential' reactions to the client from our reactions that seem objectively related to the client in some way. This discrimination is sometimes difficult to make and is daunting in any case. Correspondingly, beginning counsellors, especially, are reluctant to deal with experienced negativities about themselves in relation with the client but it is never easy even for experienced counsellors. It is also difficult to hide such reactions, however. Clients may sense counsellors' struggles even when attempts are made to keep them hidden. Moreover, because of deference, clients are reluctant to express the impact of their counsellors' insecurities. The result may be that counselling may drag on, with neither party being happy with it. The counselling may quietly be in crisis.

Alternatively, when counsellors disclose their inner feelings concerning the relationship with the client, seeming paradoxes may ensue. The counsellor may feel more empowered, rather than weakened, by the transparency. After all, in being transparent, counsellors are at one with their experience and their expression of it – they are congruent. Besides, when the transparency has to do with the counsellor's disclosure of insecurities, the client often feels closer to the counsellor because the latter is admitting what the client sensed all along. On the other hand, when the transparency has to with the client's insecurities, although painful, it often rings true and may set the stage for more meaningful self-exploration by the client.

Transparency has many similarities to counsellors' disclosure of reactions to the client which is the hallmark of the interpersonal approach to counselling/therapy. As with interpersonal therapists, counsellors using the current approach are encouraged to view their negative reactions to the client as *not* necessarily subjective and correspondingly to feel empowered to voice them, especially when it seems that counselling is going nowhere. At the same time, there is a somewhat lesser tendency in the current approach to assume that negative reactions are probably objective, which opens the door to a comparatively more frank discussion of the real, as opposed to transferential, relationship.

7
Process Identification and Process Direction

By the term 'process' I am referring to the activities in which clients engage as they work with their experience from moment-to-moment. The activities may be cognitive or behavioural. There are many cognitive activities signified in our vocabulary, such as remembering, anticipating, attending, considering, reconsidering, deliberating, reasoning, concentrating, discriminating, integrating, clarifying, realizing, struggling, characterizing, rehearsing, imagining, speculating, fantasizing, creating, conceptualizing, supposing, hypothesizing, hoping, believing, doubting, challenging, confronting, deciding, re-deciding, planning, scheming, manipulating, evading, resisting, denying, substituting, displacing, dissociating, and so on. Notice that all of these terms are gerunds. Accordingly, cognitive processes are represented linguistically by verb forms. These cognitive activities can have any object. Thus, the act of considering something, for example, may have to do with the client's partner, job, project or counsellor. So too with all of the other activities.

Alternatively, activities may be behavioural in addition to whatever cognitive activities are involved with them. Thus, for example, a man may withdraw emotionally from his wife while trying to give no outward sign, or he may both distance in this way and sleep on the couch.

Treating the processing as an object

As mentioned, when we engage in activity, whether cognitive or behavioural as well, we operate within a felt-sense. The felt-sense is the 'sounding board' that guides our activity. When the felt-sense is basically friendly (a way of putting it that we owe to Gendlin) or at least promises to be so, we act either in terms of it, such as when it is enjoyment, or in pursuit of what it promises to be, as in satisfaction. When in this state, it is as if we are pulled by the felt-sense. Alternatively, it may not be friendly, in which case we may act in ways that allow us to avoid it. Now, the state that we are in, or want to be in, may be more regnant than our awareness of our activity. Thus, when writing this paragraph, I have a felt-sense of whether or not I seem to be getting right whatever it is I am trying to say. That sense is strong; what is less strong is the realization that I am engaged in the activity of composing. Indeed, that word only came to me in the instant that I thought I might try to use my immediate experience as an example of what I am trying to say.

Becoming aware of our activity in this way may, in turn, alter the felt-sense associated with it. For example, prior to my realization that I am composing, I felt a little tense; I was caught up in wanting to get what I am trying to say right, to get to the point where I would know that I've *done* it. Yet, when I realized that I'm composing, the tension let up a little. Composing something is an act of creativity; in creativity uncertainty is inherent. Reminding myself of this eased the pressure, as did the coinciding memory that past projects of this sort somehow got done so long as I persevered.

Not only may becoming more aware of our activities associated with felt-sense alter it, the awareness may also impact on the actitivies themselves. For instance, in realizing that I am composing, I am now in a position to take stock of how I have just gone about doing my composing. I remember that I have been discarding an earlier draft. Perhaps I should re-read that draft to see if some of it should be incorporated after all. Perhaps I should make an outline. Or take a break.

This is an example of dealing with a friendly felt-sense. As an illustration of the opposite, let us take procrastination. Here the felt-sense is one of not wanting to do whatever it is that needs to be done. It is a heavy feeling, oppressive; the thought of actually starting up to do it makes us feel uncertain, anxious, even panicky. To control those negative feelings we separate ourselves from what it is that we need to do. We put it in a corner somewhere, less in mind. We still feel it but the feeling is muffled. Every now and then we allow ourselves to actually think about what we need to do and are seized by another anxiety attack, and we put the thought back in the corner. We can do all of this without clearly realizing what it is that we are doing. We are only dimly aware that we are refusing to think about it clearly, that we have neither decided to do it nor not to do it, that when we do think about it we dismiss it as quickly as possible in order not to be tormented by the pain of it. Again, we are much more aware of what we are feeling, want to feel, or do not want to feel than we are of what we are doing in relation to such feeling states.

There is another reason why the felt-sense is more apparent than the activity associated with it. This has to do with the immediacy of the felt-sense compared with cognitive activity. The felt-sense is a presence that is always there *as* we think. It seems separate from thinking, somehow. Unless we direct our attention to it, we may not know just *how* we are feeling, in the sense that we have not put a label on it, but we feel it all the same. The feeling flows along with our thinking. We refer to it as we go; we are guided by it. Thinking is different. As claimed, we cannot simultaneously think something and be aware of thinking it. We just do it. This means that, in order to become aware of how we are thinking, we have to stop it to examine it. We have to break out of the intention-in-action in which we are engaged and pay attention to it, which means that it is now the activity in which we have just been engaged. Accordingly, to do that is to stop the flow within our felt-sense and which is pulling us forward. It seems to defeat our purpose. Yet, in the interest of processing our experience more effectively, being reflexive in this way is perhaps exactly what we should do because, once we are aware of what we have just done, it opens up possibilities of other ways of doing whatever it is that we are doing. This is where process identification comes into play in counselling.

Process identification

Process identification is the counsellor's activity of drawing clients' attention to what they are doing. The activity addressed in this way may be either cognitive or behavioural because either form of activity may be in the background of clients' awareness as they dwell in the meaning of their experience – meaning that has much to do with their felt-sense. Prior to this consideration of process, in this book I have addressed the importance of understanding and helping clients to understand the meaning of their experience. This is empathy and empathic responding. In process identification, we shift our attention away from the meaning of clients' experience of meaning to the activity in which they are engaged *as* they experience that meaning. Going back to the example of procrastination, let us say that clients for whom procrastination is a problem spend time in counselling narrating incidents having to do with once again putting off doing work. There may be many meanings at play, a lot to do with feeling. In reaching across to this experience, we may be prompted to give empathic responses such as, 'It was a dismal moment. You were feeling that you really *must* get down to it, yet just couldn't seem to do it.'

Alternatively, we may pay attention to what clients are doing *in* conveying their experience. What are they doing? A couple of things. First of all, they are *remembering* an incident of procrastination. Secondly, they are *narrating* the memory, telling a story. Thus we have the option of either making the observation, 'You're remembering another time when you procrastinated.' Or 'You're telling a story of how you procrastinated.' Notice the subtle difference when compared to the empathic response. The latter is supportive and may also help clients to move deeper into the feeling-sense surrounding the procrastination. The process identification, in contrast, is a little confrontational, even when said in a light and friendly way. It draws their attention to whatever they are doing, to put it in the form of a concept. As a concept, it has meaning only when compared with something else. Thus, once clients realize that they are remembering, or narrating, as the case may be, they are prompted to compare that activity with something else that might be done. They might then realize that they are *only* remembering or narrating. Going with this 'only' may be a flood of new realizations – some good, some bad. On the good side, it may be realized that it is useful to tell stories in this way because it gets the feelings out and because it helps to get one's thinking straight (Rennie, 1994c). On the bad side, it may be realized that the remembering and narrating has amounted to little more than whinging, that it is passive, that it has not really involved intending to *do* anything about it.

Notice that such self-reflections are very meaningful in their own right and, moreover, that this meaning is not detached from the meaning experienced prior to our intervention. Instead, the latter is put in a new light. Our procrastinating clients may realize that what they have been doing probably had to do with self-pitying as much as anything else and, going with that, with feeling powerless, helpless. The process identification has given them a little jolt; it may stimulate them to think about intervening in the difficulty instead of merely reporting on it.

In this example, I have focused on cognitive processing. We can also draw attention to gestures accompanying their discourse. When clients characteristically look directly at us when discoursing but, in a particular moment, avert their gaze, we may remark, 'You looked away as you said that.' There are many such gestures that can be drawn to the client's attention, such as 'You hesitated just there.' Or, 'You sighed as you said that.' Or, 'You're pumping your foot up and down as you say this. Did you notice that?' Or,

'I notice that your arms are crossed as you're saying this.' Or, 'Your shoulders dropped just now.' Gestures are often expressions of covert or tacit intentions behind communication. Gaze aversion may signal an intention to hide communicatively from the counsellor; hesitation may be a sign of discarding of one thought in exchange for another; foot pumping with a reluctance openly to express tension of some sort; arm crossing with an intention to withhold information, or feelings, or both; and so on. When we notice a gesture through a process identification, we often have the effect of liberating the client to disclose the covert intentionality, thereby opening up a new line of meaning. Following Perls's lead, gestalt therapists know well the usefulness of process work of this sort, maintaining that people can control their language more easily than their gestures.

Deciding when to use process identifications

When combining empathic work with process work, our life as counsellors gets more complicated because we have to be aware of two things about the client rather than one. When empathic, we are attuned to what the client is saying and feeling; now we have to be aware of what they are doing as well. This is not as difficult as it may seem, however. The content of the client's experience is potentially very large indeed, but the number of processes involved in experiencing is not. While paying attention to what the client is saying and the manner in which it is being said, we still have time to ask ourselves: 'What is he (or she) doing now?' The answer may not come to us immediately but, over the course of the moments in which the client is doing whatever it is he or she is doing, we may have an answer. For that matter, if we feel it is important to ascertain just what it is that the client *is* doing, we can always ask for help in trying to sort it out: 'I can't quite get a sense of what you're doing right now. Are you speculating, or coming up with a realization, or . . . ?'

Identifying the activity in which clients are engaged is one thing, knowing when to comment on it is another. Being greeted with a process identification also gives clients more to take into account. Now they, too, have to think of two things rather than one. If they are to cling to the track that they are on, then they have to consider the implications of the activity, to which their attention has been drawn, for the complex of felt-sense that they have just been addressing. Hence, the flow of their tracking may be impeded, at least to a small extent and for the moment. The flow may take on new meaning in the light of the intervention (which is what we would hope), but it will require extra work for this to happen. For example, the client might say, 'As I think about it, it doesn't make much sense.' An empathic response might be, 'It's confusing.' Alternatively, a process identification might be something like, 'You're considering it and, as you do so, you're discovering that it doesn't add up.' The difference is subtle but it may be important. The empathic response is targeted on the experience and designed to deepen the client's contact with it. The process identification does this in part but is more designed to alert the client to the activity or activities that were engaged in addressing the experience.

If clients seem to be making progress in response to our empathic responding, then it is generally best to leave well enough alone. Still, process identifications may be helpful when used occasionally. They may shake clients up a little but that is not necessarily a bad thing. It gives them something else to think about; it stimulates them to put things into a new perspective. Thus, when receiving empathic responding generally works well for clients, we may slip in a process identification every now and then, just to make things more interesting.

Alternatively, we may want to draw upon process identifications because we are not satisfied with the returns from empathic responding. Interestingly, the clue to such dissatisfaction often comes from our reaction to the client, interpersonally. Feeling bored, frustrated, irritated or 'put upon' may be signs that he or she is not making much headway. Thus, in the case of a 'procrastinating' client, while listening we may be feeling that we've heard all this before, that the client is whinging, spinning wheels, and so on. We feel like we want to 'shake things up'. This might be a sign that a process identification is in order.

We may also occasionally meet clients who do not like empathic responding because it is threatening; it brings them too close to their feelings (Watson and Greenberg, 1994). Process identification is then handy because it allows clients to steer more clear of their feelings (at least in their discourse), yet it relates meaningfully to their experience and contributes to the development of a working alliance. By the same token, in this circumstance, we need to be careful about using process identifications as ways of drawing attention to gestures, bearing in mind the connection between gestures and unvocalized feelings. It is much safer to identify activities that are obvious from what the client is saying.

Descriptive and interpretive process identifications

Just as empathic responses can either stay tightly with the client's language or add an interpretive edge in a bid to enhance clients' awareness of their experience, so process identifications may be either basically descriptive or more interpretive. Thus, in the above example, when the client has said, 'As I think about it . . . ', we may take that at face value with, 'You're considering it . . . ', or we may add in an interpretive edge with, 'You're beginning to consider it . . . '. The 'beginning to' is a judgement that we are adding to what the client has said. It has a different meaning than does just 'considering'. It has historical significance. It is indicating to the client that this is something new. Correspondingly, it may be experienced by the client as tacit praise. It also has significance for the future. It suggests that, because the thinking-about-it is only just beginning, more thinking will be required in order to resolve the confusion. In this way, then, through interpretive process identifications, we can gently lead the client into further activity – just as, in interpretive empathic responses, we gently lead the client into further feeling-senses. When we alternate between empathic and process identificatory responses, we contribute to the expansion of the client's frontier on both fronts.

Immediate and historical process identification

When making a process identification, we can address either the activity in which clients are currently engaged or a past activity to which they are now referring. The first type of response may be called immediate process identification and the second historical process identification. It is the first that is used more frequently and which is most important as well. In order to avoid the frequent use of a cumbersome term, I shall use the term 'process identification' as a short form of immediate process identification.

As an illustration of the difference between the two types, let us imagine that a client says, 'I have been thinking about our session last week. When I left, I was a little tense because I wasn't sure that I could carry out my resolve or not. However, I caught myself faltering and managed to get a grip on myself before I lost the resolve altogether, and was actually able to follow through.' The activity being addressed by the client occurred in the past. A historical process identification might be something like, 'You successfully managed to resist suppressing your awareness of your resolve, and were able to convert the resolve into action.' Alternatively, the client's current activity is his recollection of the earlier activity. Thus, if we were to make a process identification (i.e. an immediate one), we might remark, 'You're remembering how you dealt with the resolve that you carried away from the last meeting.' Other choices would be 'You're reporting on . . .', 'You're pointing out . . .', or 'You're indicating . . .'. These would be descriptive process identifications. A more interpretive one would be, 'You're consolidating . . .'. If we were inclined to offer to the latter, but were unsure, we could offer it tentatively with something like, 'You seem to be – what? Consolidating how you

---

Box 7.1
Analysis of counsellor's dialogue in terms of empathic responding and types of process identification

Client	I don't know what things are bothering me. But I don't know [pause] I guess I can't [pause] I [pause] I don't know.
Counsellor	You haven't been able to connect it to anything, sort of. [**historical process identification**]
Client	It drives me nuts.
Counsellor	It's hard to talk about. [**empathy**]
Client	I felt like crying at first, but nothing would [pause].
Counsellor	Ever since the bird died, or [pause]. [**empathy**]
Client	Yeah, but it's not – like, I can connect that.
Counsellor	So, it's not – you don't think that it's connected with that, particularly? [**empathy**]
Client	Yeah. Like especially today [pause]. I keep wondering if it's connected to self-pity.
Counsellor	So you sort of doubt yourself? [**empathy, close to historical process identification**] So at the same time you feel bad but you're also saying to yourself, 'I shouldn't be feeling bad'. You're fighting yourself all the time. [**empathy and historical process identification**]
Client	Yeah. Like, there's nothing – Well, this is always a question of school but nothing has happened that is that's – I don't know – It should make me feel depressed. And it's not depression. Like, I feel kind of –
Counsellor	Agitated. [**empathy**]
Client	Yeah. I don't know why. Like, – uh, – I don't – I don't know. Like this morning I was putting my make-up on and I started crying.
Counsellor	Just sort out of the blue. There you were – [long pause]. So, because you can't find reasons for it, then – I mean really apparent reasons – you really jump on yourself. [**empathy and historical process identification**]

Process identification and direction

managed to successfully carry out the resolve that you carried away from last meeting? Something like that? Or are you doing something different here?' This last response is long-winded and diverting, and we would not want to respond like this unless we were trying to stimulate the client really to wrestle with the concept of consolidation.

There is more overlap between historical process identification and empathic responding than there is between (immediate) process identification and empathic responding. Both historical process identification and empathic responding involve a reflection of the content of what the client has said. I like to make a distinction between the two, however, because in historical process identification we are explicitly drawing clients' attention to the part of content that had to do with their agency.

To exemplify further the difference between empathic responding, process identification and historical process identification, let us go back to the transcript of the session with the young woman who talked about her self-pity (Chapter 4). I will once again turn to that excerpt but this time will indicate my sense of which of these three types of response the counsellor used (Box 7.1). In this dialogue, there are what I have judged to be historical process identifications that look rather like regular ones. The reason for the judgement is that the counsellor's responses address past activity, even though the counsellor is using the present tense.

Next, I have reconstructed parts of this dialogue by changing the counsellor's responses into process identifications (Box 7.2). In this reconstruction, I have altered only the counsellor's dialogue, leaving the client's dialogue intact. Hence, the reconstructed dialogue is not meant to represent what the client's responses might have looked like in reply to the process identifications. Instead, it is designed merely to illustrate the process identification style. Interestingly, even when the process identifications in Box 7.2 are grafted onto the original responses by the client, there is still a reasonably good flow to the resulting dialogue. Thus, even (immediate) process identifications address the content of the client's experience because they are integral to it.

The impact of process identification

Different change dynamics are set in motion by empathic and process identificatory responding. Empathic responses stimulate clients to trust and accept where they are at with themselves in a

> *Box 7.2*
> **The counsellor's dialogue converted into process identifications**
>
> *Client*   I don't know what things are bothering me. But I don't know – I guess I can't – I – I don't know.
> *Counsellor*   You are implying that things are bothering you, but you're not able to go beyond that.
> *Client*   It drives me nuts.
> *Counsellor*   And now you're focusing on how it makes you feel.
> *Client*   I felt like crying at first but nothing would [pause].
> *Counsellor*   You're remembering feeling like crying, but can't seem to take it further than that.
> *Client*   Yeah. I don't know why. Like, – uh – I don't – I don't know. Like this morning I was putting my make-up on and I started crying.
> *Counsellor*   You're recalling an incident of crying, and when you do you're realizing that the incident baffles you.

given moment, from where they take steps into unexplored territory in themselves. As indicated above, however, feelings are usually more regnant than awareness of what we are doing. Meanwhile, empathic responses have more to do with clients' feelings than with their activities. In being empathic, then, we may inadvertently draw clients' attention even further into feeling at the expense of awareness of activity. Process identifications help to correct that imbalance. In drawing attention to what they are doing, we remind clients that they *are* acting, that they are indeed capable of action (something that depressed clients, especially, lose sight of). In turn, once made aware of their activity, they are in a position to appraise it, even to engage in activities alternative to it.

As indicated, some clients hurt so much that empathic responding is difficult to deal with; in this state, they may find process identifications more manageable. These clients may then be able to work from process identifications into being able to benefit from empathic responding, by virtue of gradually beginning to experience the comfort and protection of the relationship with the counsellor. Alternatively, when clients have deeply shielded themselves from their feelings, process identifications may be useful in helping them to recognize what they are doing with themselves and may possibly pave the way for the beginning of contact with feelings. It may also be the case, however, that more than process identification is needed. They may need process direction, such as teaching them how to use Gendlin's technique of focusing on what they are experiencing.

Summarizing this section on process identification, this type of response presents to clients what they have just done while processing their experience. It indicates that they *have* just done it. It implies that any further work is similarly to be done by them (rather than the counsellor/therapist). It conveys that we believe that they can do it, both in present and future interactions. It reminds them of the appropriate locus of responsibility for change.

Process direction

Thus far in this chapter, I have dwelt upon the dual awareness that we maintain when being both empathic and process identificatory. There is yet a third awareness that we have and which we can cultivate – our evaluation of the client's processing. Depending on the circumstance, we may judge that it would be useful for the client to do more of a present activity, less of it, or an alternative activity, and we act on the judgement by suggesting that the client act accordingly.

It is the act of process *directing* that most clearly separates this experiential person-centred approach from the literal approach. When process directing, counsellors take charge. They assume the role of expert – an expert on process. In keeping with the experiential therapies, in this approach to person-centred counselling it is held that there are times when clients need help in dealing with themselves. The help has to do with how they are dealing with themselves, not what they are dealing with. Nevertheless, process direction is a clear statement of our sense of the adequacy of the client's agency. Some clients may welcome this additional agency. Others may be restive about it for any number of reasons. Being confronted with the message that their own agency is not fully adequate may threaten the self-esteem of some; for others the activity or activities suggested may threaten to move them into unwanted feelings. Thus, process directiveness has a great deal to do with the working alliance and must be negotiated, especially when it is remembered that clients have a strong tendency to defer to us. Particularly when introducing process direction, it is very important to offer it tentatively, giving the client lots of room to resist or modify suggested approaches. In the language of Bordin's (1979) notion of the working alliance, it is important to maintain the bond with the client while sorting out the task.

In this approach to counselling, the process directiveness is less technical than the directiveness characterizing more explicitly experiential approaches. As seen, the cognitive processes in question are signified by verbs in our everyday language, and the task set before clients is to do either more or less of these ordinary activities. Thus, the client may be encouraged to think more about something, to dwell more in a given memory, to try to look at something in a different way, to isolate the most significant element in a story just told and to attend more fully to what it means, to focus on the feelings associated with a given thought, and so on. It is person-centred as much as experiential because it is directing a process that is more coincident with the flow of the client's experiencing than is typical of the comparatively more structured tasks of the experiential therapies. By the same token, the present approach is a bridge to such task-work.

As an illustration of process direction in the present approach, let us continue to apply the transcript produced by the self-pitying client and her counsellor. This time I will isolate a single response by the client. In what follows, I reiterate the actual empathic response given by the counsellor, repeat my earlier process identification response, and then invent a process directive response that could have been used instead (Box 7.3).

Box 7.3
Reconstructed dialogue illustrating process direction

Counsellor   You're remembering feeling like crying, but can't seem to take it further than that.
Client   Yeah. I don't know why. Like, – uh – I don't – I don't know. Like this morning I was putting my make-up on and I started crying.
Counsellor   It seems like both the source and the nature of your feelings are unclear. I'm wondering if it might be useful to concentrate on those feelings to see if something comes up? **[process direction]**

In the last response in Box 7.3, the counsellor suggests how the client might work with her experience. This type of response does a number of things. First, in being given tentatively, it gives the client the chance to resist the suggestion or to modify it in some way. Second, it gives the client the sense that the counsellor is really working with the former's experience. Again, just how that sense plays out for the client has to be teased out, perhaps through metacommunication. Finally, the response suggests to the client a new way of dealing with her experience.

I return to process direction later in the chapter, when presenting some actual discourse that involved empathic, process identificatory and process directive responses. Before doing that, however, I want to turn to the matter of learning how to respond in terms of clients' processes.

Learning to do process identification and process direction

I have found that counsellors sometimes have difficulty when learning how to address clients' processing of experience. Part of it has to do with the difficulty imposed by the comparatively greater complexity of process work. This requires a different attentional set than does empathic work. In the latter, we are focused on how clients feel and on what they mean, and respond accordingly. In process identification, we are aware of feelings and meanings and of what the client has just done; in process direction, we are aware of all three – and of what the client might do as well.

When shifting from relating to feelings and meanings to relating to clients' process, we experience a shift of feeling within ourselves. When being empathic, we are to a certain extent living within the feelings of clients. This gives us a sense of being connected with them. When shifting from empathic to process responding, the object of our attention is no longer clients' feelings but instead their activities and, correspondingly, the feeling-connection with clients is broken to a certain extent. What they are feeling and meaning is still present in us but these aspects are no longer figural; for the moment, they have receded into the background.

When being initiated into process work, counsellors often worry that this relatively detached way of responding will alienate them from their clients. It may take a while for them to realize that what clients do is just as much a part of them as what they are feeling or meaning and that working with clients' activities connects us with them as well, although in a different way than does empathic responding.

In any case, when learning the approach, counsellors may feel a subjective barrier in the way of shifting to the process mode. In overcoming the barrier, the biggest step is to break away from the feeling-connection with the client, and its corresponding attention to what the client is saying, to what the client is doing. The shift can be done in two ways. The first is to make this switch completely. This way of being with clients is simple; we are now paying more attention to one thing as opposed to the other, and conversing accordingly. And, indeed, as indicated above when referring to clients who seem to have difficulty with empathic responses, there may be times when we would want to respond in this way. The second way is to blend empathic and process responding, and this is usually the most useful way. Here we are mainly empathic but in brief spaces between empathic attention and responding we attend to what the client is doing. Clients give those spaces to us, as pauses in their discourse.

When starting out with this kind of work, it is useful to ask ourselves during pauses, 'So, what is he (or she) doing now?' After doing this for a while, the explicit question no longer becomes necessary; the interest in what the client is doing becomes ongoing and, in any given moment, we may decide to act on it. In the same vein, when first starting out, it gets us over the barrier between thinking about clients' process and actually responding in terms of it if we use the prompt, 'So, what you're doing now is . . . '. Saying this may seem awkward but it often does not sound especially so to clients, because they usually hear whatever we say within the rush of their own thoughts. After a while, just as we no longer need to think the sentence as a way of getting ourselves habitually interested in process, so too we get to the point where we no longer have to use the lead-in when drawing clients' attention to what they are doing. At that point we feel more comfortable in switching from empathic responding by moving directly to an observation such as, 'You're remembering . . . ', or 'You're realizing . . . '.

Some dialogue between a former client and myself, reported in Box 7.4, illustrates movement back and forth between empathic and process responses; there is also an instance of metacommunication. The exchange in Box 7.4 is fairly typical of process work.

Box 7.4
Real dialogue illustrating empathic responding, process identification and direction, and metacommunication

Counsellor I heard you say that you went to the group because of one person.
Client Just because I was friends.
Counsellor I see.

Process identification and direction 85

Client	I knew one person pretty casually.
Counsellor	Mm hm, I see. So then, it's when you're with people with whom you're not familiar that the pressure gets really intense. [empathy]
Client	Right.
Counsellor	Mm hm.
Client	Where I feel real threatened.
Counsellor	Can you identify what it is about that, that's so threatening? [process direction]
Client	I want to look good in their eyes. I want me to look good.
Counsellor	Even though you don't mean anything to them. [empathy]
Client	Yeah. I, uh, yeah.
Counsellor	You're smiling at that. [process identification]
Client	Well, they do mean something to me. Not as a friend, but [pause]. Huh! I don't even know what they do. Maybe it's just for my own self-esteem.
Counsellor	Would you like to examine that for a moment? [process direction]
Client	Uh. [pause]
Counsellor	Did the way I phrased that tend to stop you? [metacommunication]
Client	Yeah.
Counsellor	Yeah. All right. Can I try again? [metacommunication]
Client	Sure.
Counsellor	How does self-esteem enter into it? [empathy and tacit process direction]
Client	OK. That's better [chuckles]. Uh, well there's no reason why I should want to look good in their eyes . . .
Counsellor	Mm hm.
Client	for any other reason than that I should want them to see me as being good. And the only reason why I should want them to see me as good and intelligent, or whatever, is so I can feel better. Because if I really felt that I was good, then the threat wouldn't be there. They wouldn't see it. If they wouldn't see it, then that would be their mistake.
Counsellor	Mmmmf!
Client	So (unclear) reassurance.
Counsellor	Yeah. So we're again back to, uh, defining yourself in terms of other people's expectations of you. [historical process identification]
Client	Yeah. In this situation – it's a threatening situation, and I think all people would feel threatened. But I'm definitely kind of accentuating it. [Pause]
Counsellor	So, does all consideration of that stop there, or does it lead to anything? [empathy]

Client	It leads to, again the fact that I can recognize why I feel that way, and what situations make me feel that way. If I could take the time to think why I feel that way, it would again give me the choice of acting in a role of acting as myself. In a situation where I feel threatened, the important thing would be to think it through. That would give me the choice. [Pause]
Counsellor	So [pause] I don't know how to phrase this. [**metacommunication**] What would be required of you to be able to do that? Or, how would you do that? Or could you do that? [**process direction**]
Client	The first step would be to recognize when I feel that way.
Counsellor	When you feel threatened?
Client	Right.
Counsellor	Yes. [**empathy**]
Client	And identify why.
Counsellor	Yes. Now, let's just stop there. [**process direction**]
Client	OK.
Counsellor	Could you go about identifying how you feel threatened? [**process direction**]
Client	I know when I, uh – it's a feeling in my stomach. I get a [pause].
Counsellor	Can you describe that feeling? [**process direction**]
Client	It's like really intense butterflies. Really, uh. [pause]
Counsellor	Intense butterflies. Do you mean almost nauseous? [**empathy**]
Client	Mmm. Yeah. [chuckles, then pauses] A little.
Counsellor	Not to the point where you want to throw up? [**empathy**]
Client	No. But [Counsellor interrupts]
Counsellor	It's a churning. [**empathy**]
Client	Yeah, it's a churning. It churns. I don't feel nauseous, but I do feel sick to my stomach.
Counsellor	Mmm. It's that strong. [**empathy**]
Client	Oh, yeah. Yeah. At times. Definitely.
Counsellor	That's a pretty strong cue. [**empathy**]

The counsellor directs the client to do something that the counsellor thinks might be helpful. Once the client resolves the problem posed by the counsellor and proceeds to derive a new realization, the counsellor empathically conveys understanding and support of the realization. We are given a glimpse into the client's reaction to the exchange during an Interpersonal Process Recall (IPR) enquiry into it (Box 7.5).

> **Box 7.5**
> **Client's commentary on the dialogue in Box 7.4**
>
> *Client*   I don't know how he figured it – (how) he picked it up. He asked me if I knew how to identify when I feel threatened, and that led to the rest of the whole session. It was really important and it allowed me to focus on and be able to identify when I feel threatened and how to deal with it. Again, I don't know how he picked out that certain thing but it turned out to be really important.
> *Researcher*   So, somehow or other he picked out a focus that was really important that you might have missed if you hadn't done that.
> *Client*   Yeah, it was something that I knew about but never thought about, and I would never have focused on it. He just asked me a direct question about how I feel at the moment and I was able to express it and because of it, it helped to feel a lot more comfortable in the situation. It helped me to feel more comfortable opening up.

In this commentary we have evidence of the dividends that can result from giving clients direction on how to work with their experience. Moreover, there is also a suggestion that the direction may not necessarily feel coercive. In this instance at least, the client reported that what I had done had *allowed* him to focus; he did not say that it had forced him to do so. A feature of this particular process direction is that it was akin to those made by gestalt therapists in that it directed the client to attend to the immediacy of the situation in question, which led to an identification of pertinent bodily sensations; in short, the client got out of his mind and into his body. Once there, he became explicitly aware of what had hitherto been non-reflexive. More generally, the exchange is a good illustration of the way, in process work, we focus on *how* clients deal with themselves rather than on the content of their experience. Once this is done, new and significant content may emerge.

Summary

In this chapter, I have defined the term 'process' as the ways in which we deal with ourselves from moment-to-moment. The activities in question are cognitive and behavioural. We tend to be more aware of our felt-sense, and going with it the meaning of our experience, than we are of what we are doing that is associated with our experience. In the counselling situation, empathic responding is a way of working with clients' felt-senses as they deal with the meaning of their experience. This way of being with clients is very useful as long as it contributes to their movement as they search for meaning and ways of dealing more effectively with their lives; indeed, this approach may be generally sufficient for some clients. An alternative way of being with clients is to draw their attention to their processing of experience, either in terms of what they are doing here and now or in terms of what they have done in the past, and/or to direct their processing. Compared with empathic responding, it may give clients a new perspective on their experience and may stimulate them to realize new ways of dealing with it. At the same time, process work is not divorced from empathic responding. Rather, it emerges from such responding and returns to it. The balance between empathic and process responding that is achieved, from moment-to-moment in the counselling exchange, is a matter for counsellors to decide, depending on their sense of what would be useful to the client.

The use of the concept of clients' processing in the present chapter has been limited to their relationships with themselves, either in terms of those relationships *per se* or in terms of their relationships with others in terms of their relationships with themselves. In this sense, the focus has been on clients' intrapsychic experience. There is another process going on in counselling as well, of course, to do with the interpersonal relationship between clients and their counsellors. I have touched on this aspect from time to time thus far when addressing metacommunication. It is now time to address metacommunication more fully.

8
Metacommunication

In the evolution of consciousness, reflexivity gave rise to communication (Donald, 1991) and complicates it in that we can exert control on our communication in order to suit our wishes. Thus, we can say one thing while thinking another, we can say it with this or that tone, we can say with or without gesture, we can say it *as* gesture, and we can decide not to say it at all. Moreover, this complexity goes on in a context and the meaning of what we say or do not say makes sense only in that context. All this is not to say that we have total control over how we communicate. Our feelings often get in the way of control and we may communicate by how we look and behave, regardless of how much we try to control ourselves.

Let us look at the counselling situation and, to make our language easier, let us assume that both the counsellor and client are female. In this situation, each partner in the exchange is present to herself and represents that presence to herself. Each also represents herself to the other. When the individual's self-representation is the same as her self-presence (i.e. as her 'experiencing'), as near as she can determine, then the individual is congruent. When the individual represents herself congruently to the other, then the individual is transparent. It is when congruence and transparency are missing that difficulties arise. In the first instance, the individual has difficulty understanding herself; in the second, the other has difficulty understanding her. Notice that all of this is symmetrical; it applies as much to the client as to the counsellor.

By paying close attention to context, to the manner and tone with which the client says things, to the gestures given, to what is not said as well as what is said and to the client's body language, the person in the role of counsellor empathically seeks to understand the one in the role of client and, correspondingly, to stimulate her to achieve greater self-understanding. In turn, this increased self-understanding may be associated with increased agency. Alternatively, the counsellor may engage in process work to promote agency, which in turn may be associated with increased self-understanding. Meanwhile, the person in the role of client is trying to understand the counsellor by paying attention to what she says, how it is said, her gestures, her body language and what she is not saying. Just like the counsellor, the client uses all of these cues as ways of filling in the gaps between what the other person is saying and what she seems to mean.

Despite the use of all of these cues, however, the meaning that is gleaned by the receiver of the other's communication is only approximate. Nor can the belief that one understands the other necessarily be trusted. Angus (Angus and Rennie, 1988) has found that, in the light of tape replay-stimulated recall of clients' and counsellors' experiences of the same moments of exchange having to do with metaphor, it was possible for both parties to carry on a conversation where each believed that he or she understood the other when each was on a different wavelength.

In the face of such uncertainty, it is possible to get further beneath the surface of the other's communication by enquiring into the other's sense of the meaning behind it. It is also possible to reveal to the other the meaning behind one's own communication. Such activity, in being communication about communication, has been referred to as metacommunication (Kiesler, 1982, 1996; Watzlawick, Beavin and Jackson, 1967).

In principle, metacommunication works both ways of course. The individual may enquire into what is behind the other's communication, and vice versa. In the annals of counselling theory, research and practice, however, the line of metacommunication has been mainly one-way. Thus, in classical psychoanalysis, analysts interpret to their analysands that the latter's communication is an expression of transference and/or resistance. In interpersonal psychiatry (Sullivan, 1953), the psychiatrist acts as participant-observer, confronting the client about his or her communications with others. In the behavioural and cognitive therapies, practitioners provide guidance in that respect. In Kiesler's (1982, 1996) approach to interpersonal psychotherapy, the therapist reveals to clients how their communication impacts on the counsellor. Even Rogers's person-centred counselling was one-way. Rogers was much more inclined to check on the client's impact on him and to be interested in learning more about the client's purposes; he was reluctant to ask for his impact on the client and to reveal his purposes (for purposes and impacts, see below).

As we have seen, this one-sided metacommunication is reflective of the Cartesian–Lockean dualism that has pervaded Western thought since the Enlightenment. Thus therapists in this tradition prefer to see themselves as subjects and clients as objects, themselves as agents and clients as patients. Also, going along with this, is the tendency for therapists to assume that they have more cognitive privilege than the client. Similarly, although therapists may recognize that they may react subjectively to the client (or counter-transfer), it is tacitly held that it is possible to be purged of this subjectivity, in the main, so long as appropriate steps are taken.

This is not to say that such dualism pervades the psychotherapy scene totally. Existential therapy (May, Angel and Ellenberger, 1958), the politics of experience and associated therapy advanced by Laing (1967), certain forms of interpersonal therapy and of object relations therapy (see Kiesler, 1996), and feminist therapy (see McLeod, 1993), to name a few, place the counsellor and client on a more even playing field. This is also true of the current approach, by virtue of two-way metacommunication.

Levelling the playing field: the virtue of two-way metacommunication

Some psychoanalysts, such as Greenson (1967), have pointed out that in the analytic situation three relationships are involved. There is the subjective relationship involving transference on the client's side and/or counter-transference on the psychoanalyst's side. There is the working alliance, which is the relationship pertaining to the activity of analysis. Finally, there is the real relationship, which has to do with the client's objective experience of the psychoanalyst.

Once it is taken fully into account that both clients and counsellors are reflexive, and once we grant that clients may come to know counsellors better in some respects than they know themselves, greater recognition is given to the real relationship in counselling. Going with it, the door is opened to a refined way of developing the working alliance. How this may come about is the subject of the next chapter. Before it can be addressed, however, it is necessary to look more closely at communication, particularly metacommunication.

Basically, communication is a matter of purposes and impacts (cf. Elliott et al., 1985). In order to work into this, let us simplify the matter and assume that both parties are congruent. In communicating, a person intends to impact on the other in a certain way and may indicate the purpose explicitly in the communication, in which case the other is allowed to know what the person is up to. Alternatively, the person may withhold the purpose, in which case the other has to infer it. The reverse is also true, of course. Meanwhile, the person has a sense of the impact of her communication on the other. Unless the other explicitly communicates the impact, however, the person is left to infer it. This too is symmetrical.

So far so good. What happens when we take that congruence away? We then have the following situation. The person may think she has one purpose in communicating when, without awareness, she may be enacting another. In this case, the impact that she expects to make on the other does not occur. As before, the other may not let the person know of the impact but, if the other did let the person know, she would be surprised. This is also symmetrical.

What should we do with all this symmetry in the counselling situation? Should we be as open with the client as we want the client to be with us? Should we be as much prepared to work on our incongruencies as with those of clients? Can we expect clients to engage in such symmetry? The current approach is traditional in the sense that the focus is on the client, not the counsellor. *Within* that tradition, however, we emphasize the importance of being ready to be transparent to clients as we work with their concerns. We recognize that, depending on the particular moment, it may be useful to clients to let them know what we are up to so that they do not have to demystify us, and instead have a chance to influence us if what we are up to does not agree with them in some way. We may go further and explicitly enquire into how we are impacting on them. And we acknowledge that their impact on us may have to with us rather than them.

Being this way with clients does several things. It helps to make us more human with our clients, less formidable. It allows them to feel more equal to us, less deferential, more empowered. It helps to sort out and enhance the real relationship between us and our clients. And it contributes to the development, maintenance or repair of the working alliance.

This is not to say that a heavy emphasis should be placed on metacommunication. It is indeed beyond communication and thus takes clients out of their focus on themselves exclusive of their awareness of us. If they seem to make headway in response to empathic and process responding by us, there is little if any reason to disturb the work. It is only when it seems that they might benefit from metacommunication in some way that we would want to engage in it.

There was a moment like this in a session with one of my clients, recently. It went something like my reconstruction of it in

Box 8.1. The context of this moment was that we were discussing whether or not the client had been able to hold on to the new sense that I was really on his side – a sense that had come to him two sessions before and had continued in the session previous to the one being reported here.

Box 8.1
Counsellor's metacommunicative invitation to the client to share his sense of the counsellor's impact on him

Client	For some reason, the sense that you're on my side isn't as strong today. [Pause] I don't know why.
Counsellor	Is it because of something that I have done today? Perhaps I've somehow taken you away from where you were the last time we met. Is that possible?
Client	No, I don't think so. It doesn't seem to be that.
Counsellor	Mmmm. [Pause] Since we've met today, there's been something going on in me that I haven't told you about. I'm feeling upset about something that happened to me at the university today. I'm still carrying that with me. Maybe you picked that up. Have you been feeling that I'm a bit more distant from you today?
Client	No, I haven't been feeling that.

As the client made the last remark (in Box 8.1), I looked at him intently, trying to read whether he really meant what he said. He seemed sincere; I couldn't be sure, but he seemed that way (I could have asked him, which would have been another metacommunication). Putting everything he said in this exchange together, then, he said that his reduced feeling that I was on his side was due neither to anything that I did nor to the way I seemed to be with him in this session. He was thus putting the change squarely on his shoulders, not mine. That was useful because it helped to clear the air. The other thing that happened was that, in being able to disclose my upset feelings, they eased a little and so that I was able to focus on him better. At the same time, I did not seize upon the disclosure in a bid for sympathy (or at least I tried not to, and he never gave me any in any case). That was not my intent in making the disclosure and I think he knew it. Thus, the structure of the encounter remained the same: I was still the counsellor and he was still the client. In the same vein, had he reversed roles, I would have stopped him with something like, 'In saying that I did not intend to shift the focus on myself. I just wanted you to know what I'm feeling just in case you picked it up and were affected by it in some way.' Notice that such a response would have been yet another metacommunication.

In further illustration, my research has provided a number of instances in which metacommunication was not used but probably should have been. One involved a client who was addressing her difficulty in getting along with her family, and especially her mother. In Box 8.2 I give an excerpt from a counselling session concerning this issue.

Box 8.2
An instance of a counsellor's strategy that is covertly wrestled with by the client

Client	They (i.e. the family) got the idea that I've just completely shut them out of my life and decided to make – you know – start over. And so other things, uh, like, uh, get a legitimate job and get out of doing the kind of work I'm doing now, and stuff [pause].
Counsellor	How did you help them to change that idea, though? Or did you – or did you just let them think that, or what did you do about that?
Client	That was one of the – we didn't actually talk. They just, uh, I realized at one point that, oh, they don't understand that I still want a career in [her line of work] and that I'm doing my darnedest to get back together to mend the bridge between us.
Counsellor	How do you deal with their misunderstandings about you? What do you do about that?
Client	It was just when I corrected the impressions as they came up. We never act. I never actually said, uh, you know, 'These are my plans and this is what I want to do for the next five years.' It was just that any time that some little comment was made that, uh, didn't fit in with what I was actually going to do.
Counsellor	[Interrupts] You'd correct.
Client	I'd correct that one but not [pause]
Counsellor	The whole. So you never sat down and really shared with them what you wanted in your life – not trying to help them.
Client	No, because we'd fight.
Counsellor	Well, fighting isn't sharing. Fighting is fighting. You see, we can be very unhappy with the way our parents view us, but as adults we have the responsibility, if that matters to us, to try and help them. I mean, if we want them to understand, then we are

	the only ones who can sit down and take responsibility and share ourselves with them. If you haven't done that and then you're still really upset at the way they're viewing you – well, you see, you're not being responsible enough here. Or else you've got to give up complaining about them.
Client	Yeah.
Counsellor	And my sense is because of the tension, that everyone's avoiding dealing with what is making everyone tense and so you do talk about the weather and that probably raises the tension because it feels so phoney. But the – all the things that need to be said between the two of you [the reference here is to the client's mother] aren't being said. And it's your responsibility as much as her's to, to – *share* with her. She may be right out in the cold and, and you – maybe you've left so much to her imagination as to what's going on in your life that she's made up a whole of stuff that isn't true. Now she could ask for more information but you should share some more too. And if you want to heal this relationship, obviously the onus is on you. If you want, if you want to heal, then you have to do something about taking the steps to make that happen.
Client	But sometimes when I try to say things, though, she doesn't want to listen, or she says, 'That's OK, dear,' uh, 'we'll go out and have a cup of tea
Counsellor	[Interrupts] She is brushing you off.
Client	and nice, nice cake', or something.

In this exchange, the counsellor was trying vigorously to persuade the client to communicate more effectively with family members, especially her mother. We can sense that this advice is not sitting too well with the client but, if she indeed were resistant, it came out explicitly only when she defended herself at the end. It is revealing to see what the client said about the exchange when she heard the playback of it a short while after it occurred (see Box 8.3).

Box 8.3
Client's commentary on the counsellor's strategy

| Client | The thing that was operating – Once I was – Once I sort of got sorted out into what it was – what angle she was attacking from? – I also had to deal with, 'Do I believe this?' That – sort of came in as, uh, very quickly on the heels of, 'OK. I think I know |

	where she's operating. Wait a minute! Am I going to along with this?' And then I decided, 'Well, I mean, you haven't got a very good basis to judge whether you believe in it up to this point because you've never participated in this before. You've just read about it, and that's not the real thing, so go ahead.'
Researcher	Do you think she had any sense at all that this was going on in you – in the session?
Client	She prob – she might have from the expressions on my face. My face is pretty expressive at times. Uh – she never really did anything about it. – She may have picked it up, but she may have been more interested in carrying things forward, because I was going along anyways.
Researcher	If she were to have done anything about it, what would you have preferred her to do?
Client	I would have been interested in finding out, you know, what approach this was. What the label that usually adheres to this is called. Uh – that's sort of from an intellectual point of view.
Researcher	Yes. [slight pause] Yes.
Client	Uh, I think I wanted some reassurance from her that, well, 'We can only just see if it works, if it gets us anywhere.' That, 'I would like you to try this.' I think she did this the last session we had. She had me playing the one side of myself and then the other side of myself and I was surprised at that point how well it worked. I expected going into it that – and I even said that – at the end of the session – that I'm rotten at improvising. Like, [although] I'm an actress, sort of – uh, I'm rotten at improvising. I didn't expect that to work. I'm surprised that it did and it felt as though we had gotten somewhere. And she was quite reassuring at that point, that, yes, we did get somewhere.
Researcher	I'm picking up that – even a comment that somehow indicates to you that this that you're about to try is not carved out in stone but, 'Is something that we can try and we'll see how it works' which, I guess, would have the implication that if it doesn't work then 'We might try something else.' Is that what is important to you?
Client	Because my ideas about her – one of them is that she's a kind of rigid person. I was – I suppose I was apprehensive that she might want to adhere to this system and that if I didn't feel comfortable within the system, what was I going to do. As it turned out it worked.

There are a number of interesting things about this commentary. The counsellor had impacted strongly on the client; she described it variously as an attack and as if the counsellor had been operating within a system. She had been curious about the angle that the counsellor had been coming from; the client had felt that if she had known that, she might have had a better idea of how to respond to it. Despite her uncertainty about it, she had complied with it because it was new; she had decided that it deserved a try. She had been strengthened in this decision by remembering that she had taken a similar risk recently and that it had paid off. At the same time, she saw the counsellor as a little rigid and had been worried that she might have been inflexibly imposing this system on her. She would have been comforted in this regard if the counsellor had given some sort of sign that she considered her suggestion tentative – an experiment to be tried out.

In her report, the client thus indicated two quite different things. She revealed that she had felt a lot of uncertainty and had raised inwardly a number of questions as she had dealt with the counsellor's intervention, and wished that the counsellor had made it easier for her to comply with it, even though she had decided that she would comply. Yet she also reported that compliance, in the face of similar querulousness about an earlier and different kind of intervention, had worked. So which would have been better? Would it have been better for the counsellor to let the client in on what she was doing in order to give the client a chance to express her diffidence, or was it better for the counsellor to forge ahead as she did?

My judgement is that the first would have better. The client was wasting a lot of energy dealing with the strategy – energy that could have been saved if, in the light of the discourse that metacommunication would have opened up, the client's various questions could have been answered.

Four forms of metacommunication

What might such metacommunication have looked like? Assuming that it is the counsellor who initiates the metacommunication, there are four possibilities: two pertain to the counsellor's experience and two to the client's experience. The counsellor could reveal the reasons why she is doing what she is doing; she could reveal how she is reacting to the client; she could ask the client to reveal the reasons for what the client is doing; and she could ask the client to reveal how the counsellor is impacting on her. In order to illustrate these four forms, let us retrieve part of the discourse in Box 8.2. The key part, I think, is the one just before the counsellor gives her lengthy advice to the client. I'll repeat that part of the exchange, but this time I'll create how the counsellor might have replied metacommunicatively, in terms of the four ways that I have laid out (Box 8.4).

Box 8.4
The four forms of metacommunication

Counsellor How do you deal with their misunderstandings about you? What do you do with that?

Client It was just when I corrected the impressions as they came up. We never act. I never actually said, uh, you know, 'These are my plans and this is what I want to do for the next five years.' It was just that any time that some little comment was made that, uh, didn't fit what I was actually going to do

Counsellor [Interrupts] You'd correct.

Client I'd correct that but not [pause]

Counsellor The whole. So you never sat down and really shared with them what you wanted in your life – not trying to help them.

Client No, because we'd fight.

[New – created – dialogue]

Counsellor The reason that I'm asking is that I'm wondering if you might try doing something different – might try sharing in that way, as a sort of experiment. I don't know if it's a good idea or not, but it's what's coming to mind. [**Form 1** (counsellor reveals the reason(s) for his/her communication)]

Counsellor As I listen to you describe all of this, I'm feeling a little put upon, like it's up to me to come up with a solution. [**Form 2** (counsellor reveals the impact of the client's communication)]

Counsellor I wonder: Can you tell me where you're coming from when you describe all this? What's been motivating you? [**Form 3** (counsellor enquires into the purpose behind the client's communication)]

Counsellor When I put that question to you, how do you find yourself reacting to it? What's it like for you? [**Form 4** (Counsellor enquires into the impact on the client of the counsellor's communication)]

Notice how the various ways in which the four forms of metacommunication address the covert worlds of the participants. In this case, because we have the benefit of the client's commentary on the exchange with the counsellor (Box 8.2), we know a lot about the client's inner world to do with that particular exchange and enough to know that in some respects it involved disjunctions. But that fact does not make the exchange extraordinary; research on the matter has revealed that clients often experience such disjunctions. Let us move forward from the metacommunicative discourse in Box 8.4, and pretend that it had actually been used with this client in that moment and – knowing what the client has told us about herself in the research enquiry (Box 8.3) – speculate on what might have transpired if at least some of these metacommunicative forms had been carried out.

It is clear from the client's commentary that, even though she complied with the counsellor's interventions both on this and the other occasion mentioned, she was diffident both times – seemingly because they were new to her and hence difficult to judge, more than for any other reason. Interestingly, any of the four metacommunicative forms would have given her a chance to express such thoughts, although some forms may have been better in this respect than others. We also learn from the client's commentary that she felt that the counsellor was a little rigid. It would have been difficult for her to say this to the counsellor under any circumstances (Rennie, 1994a). Nevertheless, depending on how it was done (in terms of tone and manner), a Form 4 metacommunication might be sufficiently supportive to prompt the client to be honest and open with the counsellor in this regard. Even better, if the counsellor were to lead off with a Form 2 and then follow with a Form 4 metacommunication, then the client might feel even more inclined to do so. After all, in this sequence, the counsellor confronts the client then invites a confrontation back.

Let us assume that all of this was done in one way or another and that, as a result, the following cards are dealt. The client now knows that the counsellor is experiencing her as rather passive in her relations with her family and is suggesting a more active approach, as sort of experiment. On the other side, the counsellor now knows that the client is uneasy about trying some of her suggestions because they are unfamiliar, and that the client feels the counsellor is a little rigid. A lot of air has been cleared. The counsellor is now in a position to be more sensitive to how her suggestions impact on the client, and to realize that it would be easier for the client if they were offered more tentatively and with more discussion. The counsellor is also made aware of the client's perception that she, the counsellor, is rigid. This may or may not be accurate. If it is accurate, then hopefully the counsellor can deal with it reasonably non-defensively and ease up on it. Meanwhile, knowing that the counsellor is making this effort might enable the client to be more tolerant of it. Alternatively, when discussing the counsellor's seeming rigidity, both parties might come to agree that this perception may have more to do with the client than the counsellor. In this eventuality, a new line of enquiry is opened up. The roots of that perception could be sought. Who knows? Perhaps those roots extend back to the family. In this way, then, what was previously experienced as a disjunction in the client's experience of the counselling process would become a focus of that process – and one with implications for what brought the client to the counsellor in the first place.

There are parallels between this treatment of metacommunication and its use in some forms of interpersonal psychotherapy, including Kiesler's version of it. My sense is that there has been a shift toward recognizing the role of the counsellor's subjectivity (cf. Kiesler, 1982, 1996). Yet, as the leader in interpersonal therapy, Kiesler stills tends to emphasize what I have referred to as Form 2. This stance thus upholds the doctor–patient relationship characteristic of most approaches to counselling. As indicated, the current approach shifts this balance somewhat. It is not so radical as to assign reciprocal roles to both members of the dyad. Nevertheless it does give more leeway to the possibility that the counsellor may at times be inappropriately subjective, and provides a way for the client to address directly that eventuality.

Summary

Communication involves purposes and impacts. Reflexivity enables senders of communication to choose whether or not to reveal their purposes and receivers to indicate impacts. Moreover, incongruent communicators may not necessarily be aware of their purposes and thus may be surprised by their impacts. Reflexivity thus creates the opportunity not to reveal purposes and impacts, and the obscurity is compounded when incongruence is involved. Metacommunication provides a way of accessing covert purposes and impacts. It does not necessarily unravel incongruent purposes (although it may have that effect), but at least it makes the purpose *as understood* by the sender known to the receiver, so that the receiver can understand the sender's understanding. Four forms of metacommunication are used in the present approach: the counsellor's communication of the purpose of a communication to the client; the counsellor's communication of the impact of a communication by the client; the counsellor's invitation to the client to communicate the purpose of a communication; and the counsellor's invitation to the client to communicate the impact of the counsellor's communication. These four forms of metacommunication preserve the expert–client structure of the counselling relationship in that it is the counsellor who initiates the metacommunication. At the same time, the approach allows for the possibility that the counsellor may at times be subjective in a way that is disjunctive for the client and gives the client the opportunity to address that eventuality should it occur. The four forms of metacommunication take metacommunication beyond how it is customarily practised in the most prominent form of interpersonal psychotherapy, in response to the somewhat greater recognition of the possibility of problematical subjectivity on the part of the counsellor.

Throughout the book, reference has been made to the working alliance and this reference has become more focused in the present chapter. It is now time to turn directly to this important aspect of the counselling relationship.

9
Tying it All Together: the Working Alliance

According to Luborsky (1994), the concept of the working alliance was anticipated by Freud (1912/1958). Psychoanalysts have seen the client's relationship with the analyst as both unconscious and conscious, and (ideally) the analyst's relationship with the client as conscious. The client's unconscious relationship is transferential and the analysis of the transference and other unconscious expressions constitutes the psychoanalytic method. The client's consciousness comes into play through compliance with the method; it is this second engagement that variously has been referred to as the therapeutic or working alliance (e.g. Sterba, 1934; Zetzel, 1956). More recently, as seen in Chapter 8, Greenson (1967) was prominent in advocating that the real relationship is involved as well, which has to do with the client's objective, *non*-transferential perception of the analyst. Then Bordin (1979) generalized the psychoanalytic concept of the working alliance when he proposed that it is characteristic of all forms of counselling, psychotherapy and psychoanalysis. He also suggested that the alliance is constituted of three main elements – bond, goal and task. This article stimulated a large amount of empirical investigation of the working alliance, whether in terms of Bordin's particular model of it or not (for a review, see Horvath and Greenberg, 1994).

Attempts to measure bond, goal and task have led to scales that are highly correlated (Horvath, 1994). This finding is to be expected because there is an overall rapport when the client and counsellor are working well together; everything fits. At the same time, it is useful to keep these three components in mind when considering the working alliance, as I indicate in the pages to follow.

The working alliance in experiential person-centred counselling

The concept of the working alliance was never taken up by Rogers although he touched on it indirectly when proposing that the client's contact with the counsellor is one of the six necessary and sufficient conditions for positive therapeutic change (Rogers, 1957). He did not place much stock in the idea of transference, and the notion that the client complies with the therapist's method reversed the structure of the client–therapist relationship as he saw it. Even so, there was an aloofness about his engagement with the client that parallels, in interesting ways, the aloofness of orthodox psychoanalysts. In both of these approaches the practitioner is *present* as an attentive listener (and interpreter, in the case of psychoanalysis) but *absent* as a personality. In psychoanalysis, the analyst's *presence* is required so that the analyst may become an object of the transference, while in literal person-centred counselling the counsellor's presence is necessary as a source of the conditions for growth. On the other side of the coin, in psychoanalysis the analyst's *absence* is prescribed so that the transference can emerge uncontaminated by real aspects of the analyst's personality, while in literal person-centred counselling it is called for to foster growth uninfluenced by the real aspects of the counsellor's personality. Thus, in both approaches the presence of the practitioner is important only in a technical sense. The traditional psychoanalytic position has come under attack by a number of neo-Freudians (e.g. Greenson, 1967; Spence, 1982; Stolorow and Atwood, 1992). Similarly, the literal person-centred instantiation of the technique has been criticized both outside the person-centred community, especially by Buber (see Van Belle, 1980) and R.D. Laing (see O'Hara, 1995) and from within the community (O'Hara, 1995).

Since the onset of research into the working alliance following Bordin's landmark paper, the main emphasis has been on the measurement of the working alliance *as is* in a given counselling or therapy relationship, and on assessing its relationship to outcome. Although there have been exceptions (e.g. Safran's work; see below), little attention has been paid to the forms of communication that the practitioner may use in attempts to improve the working alliance. In the current approach to counselling, however, the ontology involved and its implications for the structure of the counselling situation lead to such forms of communication. Before turning to these forms, let us review the propositions making up the ontology supporting the approach and the structure of the counselling interaction.

In terms of the ontology, it is proposed, first, that both the client and the counsellor are reflexive and that this reflexivity intrinsically involves agency. Second, cognitive activity involves a cyclical flowing in and out of the reflexive forming of intentions and the non-reflexive carrying out of intentions-in-action. Third, reflexivity gives the person a choice about whether an intention is to be openly communicated and, if so, how. Fourth, this decision is influenced by a felt-sense. Fifth, apart from reflexivity and its role in the formation of intentions-in-action, there are many non-reflexive aspects of the person's beingness including both unconscious personal contents and impersonal qualities having to do with enculturation and socialization. Accordingly, sixth, it is impossible to be totally objective in one's interaction with the world or, putting it another way, people do not have what philosophers refer to as cognitive privilege. Seventh, people have a sense of self that comes more from social interaction than from organic promptings. Finally, the person's sense of self is influenced by the here-and-now relationship with any significant other.

Regarding the structure of the counselling situation, it is assumed that even though counsellors do not have cognitive privilege they nevertheless are sufficiently unburdened by unconscious influences to be able to function in the counselling situation primarily for the benefit of the client instead of themselves. Correspondingly, second, clients see counsellors as more expert than themselves over the matters that they bring to counselling and counsellors accept this expert role. Third, in virtue of the expert–client dichotomy, clients are inclined to defer to counsellors' authority. Fourth, clients may well be in a transferential relationship with the counsellor but they may be in a real relationship as well, in that they may come to know objectively the counsellor as a person. Fifth, the client's sense of the counsellor may have to do with aspects of the counsellor about which the latter is unaware. Sixth, clients discriminatively use the counsellor's contributions. Seventh, when in a relationship with a counsellor that is problematic in some way, clients shift their attention from themselves to the relationship with the counsellor in order to deal with it, as needed. Eighth, clients may do some of the work of counselling – both on themselves and on the relationship – in private while in the presence of the counsellor. Lastly, for both clients and counsellors, the purpose behind communication to the other and the impact of communication from the other may also be held in private.

Both sets of features underlying the current approach to counselling help to explain how disruptions in the working alliance can occur and be maintained. On the other hand, from those same features it becomes apparent how good working alliances may be facilitated, maintained and, if necessary, repaired. In what follows,

I first look at how it is easy to be falsely complacent about the working alliance, to the detriment of the counselling. This consideration sets the stage for the main body of the chapter, having to do with the promotion of a good working alliance during all phases of the counselling relationship.

The danger of complacency about the working alliance

The working alliance has to do with teamwork. As Bordin suggested, working in tandem comes from a sense of a bond between the counsellor and client, the sense that they know what they want to achieve, and the sense that the way they are going about achieving the goal of counselling is a good way and agreeable to both. The teamwork is pertinent from moment-to-moment, throughout a session and throughout the course of counselling. Often the alliance is not talked about directly. Instead, the client and counsellor feel their way with each other, both sensing whether or not what is happening between them is useful, or perhaps could become useful. Each reads the other. The client pays close attention to various indications that the counsellor is competent, interested and optimistic. In turn, the counsellor is alert to signs that the client is committed to the process, comfortable with the counsellor and making headway.

The position taken in the current approach is that we need to be careful about not becoming too complacent about such indicators. There may be ruptures in the alliance (Safran, Muran and Wallner Samstag, 1994) of which the counsellor is unaware. Clients cover up their distress emanating from the counselling relationship in order to protect the relationship (Hill et al., 1993; Rennie, 1994a; Rhodes et al., 1994) and this can happen in any of the above three main temporal aspects of it.

Example

To illustrate the dangers of such complacency, let us go back to my relationship with one of my clients – 'Peter', who was mentioned in Chapter 5 (p. 57), who commented that my metaphor about islands in an ocean had been difficult to grasp and had slowed him down. This comment can now be seen as an indication of a momentary rupture in the alliance. As it turned out in the light of the IPR enquiry about that particular session, moreover, other comments made by the client to the IPR interviewer revealed that a far more serious misunderstanding between the client and me had been at play, without my awareness, and which had to do with the *formation* of a working alliance. Let's look at this misunderstanding in some detail because it indicates how easy it is to miss important cues because of prereflective assumptions.

One of Peter's main problems had been procrastination, especially about university work. More deeply, underneath the procrastination had been a concern about his deceit, both with himself and with others. He had reported that he lied a lot, and well, and that it bothered him. In the counselling session previous to the one that we focused on as part of my research, he had mentioned that he studied for half an hour per day. At the time, I had assumed he meant half an hour per day, per subject. Thus, in the session under study, when this topic came up again I implied the same thing, to which he agreed. Nevertheless, in the Interpersonal Process Recall session, he told the IPR interviewer that he had lied to me in that moment. The fact of the matter was that he had studied half an hour per day for both of the courses he was taking at the time, not for each course. He had lied because he had felt that I would be astounded if he had told me the truth, and he had not wanted me to think less of him. He went on to say that his lie had disturbed his ability to focus on himself for much of the remainder of the session. Thus, my insensitivity had caused a rupture in a particular moment that had extended to the remainder of the session in which that moment had occurred.

To make matters worse, as I came to learn, my insensitivity had not ended there. The client used the IPR session as a vehicle to point out something to me that had to do with our overall relationship and the goal of the counselling (since he knew, of course, that I would learn of what he told the recall interviewer). From the beginning of our relationship he had hoped that I would notice that he had lied to me *from time to time* and that I would challenge him about it so that he could come to terms with it. Yet, I had not noticed the lying and knew nothing of his plan. In part, I suppose I could be excused because evidently he was very good at not giving himself away, according to his later account. Apart from the subtlety of whatever cues may have been involved, however, I was not well prepared to detect them because I did not expect him to be dishonest with me. I had been naïve in this regard. The result was that, as he informed me through the vehicle of the IPR session, he had given me many chances to catch him and I had failed every time. He had reached the point where he had been about to give up on me. Meanwhile, he had been quite animated in our meetings, which I had always looked forward to: I had thought we were getting along just fine.

Once I learned about my naïveté, I renegotiated the goal and the task. We agreed that my task was to be alert to the possibility that he was not being truthful with me and to confront him about it when I thought it was happening. Interestingly, after that agreement, he insisted that he did not lie that much to me. In any event, I was generally more sceptical about what he said to me and was more prepared to be gently confronting. It may have been this subtle shift in how I interacted with him that led to a positive outcome; alternatively it may have been that admitting that he had lied to me objectified and consolidated his awareness in this regard, setting the stage for more self-control. Whatever the reason, he resolved his procrastination and went on to take a PhD degree. The point of this story is that the client had kept well hidden his discontent with me and I would probably have continued, naïvely assuming that he was being straight with me, until he finally gave up on me had it not been for the intervention of the research enquiry.

I have come to the conclusion that my lack of awareness of what had gone on with this client was not simply a case of my being an inept counsellor. Instead, it is also an example of the kind of disjunction that can occur because clients are so inclined to defer to us. Nor do I see the possibility of disjunctions in the relationship as emanating only from the client's side. In a parallel way, as counsellors we often keep from our clients indications of what *we* are up to, so that misunderstandings can result from our side too (Rhodes et al., 1994).

An IPR interview often results in the interviewee telling the recall interviewer about both the former's purposes behind communications to the counsellor and the impacts of the counsellor's communications. Notice the familiarity of this ground. Generalized to the counsellor's side as well, it is exactly what was addressed in the Chapter 8. Correspondingly then, in the present approach to counselling, metacommunication is seen as the key to establishing, maintaining and repairing the working alliance. As I shall now develop, the four forms of metacommunication can be applied to any content. Consequently, the same principles apply whether we are addressing the alliance in the moment, in the session or overall. I shall begin with the overall alliance because that will bring in the development of the alliance in the first session, which is critically important. From there I shall address the matter of goals and tasks – the backbone of the alliance – following which I shall address the moment-to-moment alliance. Finally, I will return to the overall alliance when concluding the chapter with a consideration of how productively to end the counselling relationship – an important aspect of the counselling relationship that is often ignored in texts of this sort.

The overall alliance

As foreshadowed in Chapter 2, whether or not an alliance is to be formed – and, if so, how – begins even before the first meeting. Clients enter that meeting with expectations and needs that have a direct bearing on how they are going to experience the meeting. Some clients evidently enter in great distress and launch into their troubles, while others seem wary of the whole process. As a general rule, it is best to negotiate the alliance with clients in the first state towards the *end* of the first session, and to reverse the timing with clients in the second state. For distressed clients who come in with a need to talk, metacommunicating during the main body of the meeting gets in the way of their desire to unburden themselves and disrupts the alliance that is forming by virtue of our being prepared to listen, and thus needs to be done very sparingly. Alternatively, defensive clients may not be able to focus on themselves until the counselling situation is dealt with. In either case, it is vitally important to address the alliance directly at some point in the first interview, however much it may have been attended to indirectly. Let us look first at the distressed client who is motivated to talk.

Developing the alliance with distressed clients who have a need to talk When first meeting distressed clients who have an urge to talk, our main task is to balance our desire to let them tell their stories and get out their feelings with our need to gather certain information that we feel is important (such as needing to ascertain whether or not a client worried about coping with being pregnant is indeed pregnant; see Box 4.1, p. 35). The current approach follows the literal person-centred tendency to stay out of the client's way as much as possible in the initial session, but it is not slavish in this respect. Instead we choose propitious moments, usually when clients seem at the end of dealing with a given topic, to ask questions if needed. Thus we gradually manage to make our enquiries over the course of the meeting and in a way that gives clients the sense that, in the main, they have held the floor. Admittedly, some clients will talk non-stop if allowed, in which case it may be necessary to interrupt them. In this situation, we may want to metacommunicate before the first interruption in order to explain it and ensuing interruptions. It is important to note that a metacommunication of this type is not designed to address the working alliance as a whole but rather to increase the rapport in the moment; however, it may, of course, help to prepare the ground for a more general consideration of the alliance. In the moment, then, we can soften our intrusiveness with a remark such as:

> I notice that you've got a lot to say. I'd like to simply listen, except that questions sometimes arise in me as I do so [Form 2]. For example, right now I am wondering if you have taken any steps to determine if you are actually pregnant. You may find that as we go along in the meeting, I'll butt in and ask such a question [Form 1].

I'll try not to get you too far off your track when doing so [Empathy + Form 1]. Also, it may be helpful to realize that *for me*, at least, you don't need to get everything out today [Empathy + tacit Form 2 + tacit Process Directive]. So: having said all that, what *have* you done to determine if you're actually pregnant?

The answer to a question may, or course, open up a whole new topic that demands attention, in which case the client *is* taken off track. Should we feel that the track is important to the client, we can ease the tension associated with the shift to the new topic with a metacommunicative bridge such as:

Well, it looks like we need to look at this [Process Directive], wouldn't you agree? [Form 4]. I realize that that will take us away from where you were, but we can get back to that after discussing this other matter, if you like [Form 1]. All right? [Form 4].

Moving on to the *closing* of the first meeting, regardless of how much metacommunicating we do around particular moments in the meeting, it is very important to open up a discussion toward the end of the meeting about the impact of the session as a whole, and about its implications for the future. A complete finishing of the first session is easily ignored, especially when it seems to counsellors to have gone well. Consequently, they often close with a remark like, 'Golly. I had no idea that the time had gone by so quickly; I'm afraid we must stop.'

Even when a closing of the first session like this is based on an accurate sense of the client's experience of it, a number of important considerations are left out. We need to learn about the relationship between what happened in the session and the client's expectations of it because this relationship has much to do with future considerations. Thus, a pattern of dialogue that works well is to take an opening no less than ten minutes before the end of the session to make a remark like:

I notice that we're going to have to end in a few minutes; perhaps we can take stock. I am wondering what this meeting has been like for you, whether it was what you expected or . . . [Form 4].

If the client seems a little bewildered, this can be followed with something like:

I guess what I'm saying is that I realize that this whole business of going to counselling can be pretty confusing – two people trying to reach across to each other, as it were. I'm just wondering if what we did today was sort of what you expected, or whether you would have preferred it if we'd gone about things a little differently – that sort of thing [Empathy + Form 4 + tacit Process Direction].

In response to this type of enquiry, clients generally indicate that the session went well, although their response may be qualified. If they sound convincing, then it remains to discuss whether they would like to meet again, and for how long because it is important to give them control over the matter of projected length of contact. When we leave the length of time open, it can lead them to wonder, 'What am I getting myself into here?' Thus, it is often a good strategy to suggest to them that we might meet for, say, four sessions and then review how things stand at that point. There is always the possibility, of course, that clients may falsely reassure us when we enquire into the impact of the first meeting. The way in which they respond may provide a clue as to the sincerity of their reply but, as we have seen, it may not. Thus we are always in a bit of a dilemma; if we do not make the enquiry, we leave the alliance insufficiently addressed; if we do, we run the risk of stimulating clients to say things they may regret. Nevertheless, research on the client's experience of counselling supports the conclusion that potential benefits from the enquiry probably outweigh potential costs.

Alternatively, when asked, clients may indicate in one way or another that they were not completely happy with the first meeting. The reasons for such an appraisal can be legion, of course. They may generally have to do with clients' despair that *anything* will help, or they may be about their disappointment at the way we went about the meeting. In the first case, once the scepticism has been expressed, it gives us a chance to work with it directly. Sometimes it helps to indicate simply that dealing with problems 'like this' often takes time; if clients seem to respond somewhat to this, then we can use it as a lead to agreeing to meet for three or four times before attempting to form any conclusions about the usefulness of such meetings. Should clients agree, then we have the beginning of an alliance; it is thin, but it is something, and may be enough to bring the client back so that a more complete alliance can be worked out.

On the other hand, because of deference, if clients are disappointed in our approach to the meeting, they are likely to hide it behind expressed self-doubt of some sort. However, depending on their personality and on how much they were disappointed, they may be more direct with something like, 'Oh, I don't know. I'm not sure this is going to work out.' Thus, sensitivity is required to detect covert scepticism about our approach to counselling. If we sense something along these lines is operating, we can gently probe for it with a remark like:

> I may be wrong but I'm sensing that in some way this hasn't been quite right for you. I don't know if I'm correct, and I don't know if you want to talk about it if I am, but if you can then perhaps we could work something out [Form 4].

Of course, even such an invitation may not be responded to honestly but at least we have done what we can do to make contact. On the other hand, if the invitation is successful in prompting the client to come out from behind cover then we are in a position to negotiate how we might approach the counselling in the future should the client decide to give it at least one more try. This negotiation would involve indicating in general terms our sense of our role and the client's role in counselling, doing what we can to meet the client's preferences without compromising our integrity, and suggesting a brief trial period. Should the negotiation fail, then our task is to suggest a referral. Notice that if this is the outcome of the negotiation, it is still a success because the client's needs have been kept uppermost.

The defensive client We may know in advance that some clients are likely to be defensive and possibly hostile, as when they are coerced into counselling. Alternatively, we may have no reason to expect defensiveness but discover it once clients arrive. Either way, we do not necessarily rely on reflection of the defensiveness (the literal person-centred way) or attribute it solely to transference (the orthodox psychodynamic way) or, indeed, treat it as probably transferential (the interpersonal psychotherapeutic way). Rather we address it as open-mindedly and directly as possible while keeping the focus on the client. Thus, we pick up the cues given to us and work with them metacommunicatively. Depending on our sense of the situation, we have the option of beginning with enquiries into the client's experience, with revelations of our own experience as it relates to the client's situation, or both. In the first instance, we say something like, 'I notice that you seem uncomfortable in this situation [or nervous, angry, irritated, edgy – whatever seems to fit]. I wonder if you could talk about what it's like for you to be here?' [Form 4, generalized to the impact of the counselling situation]. Or, 'I sense that it's difficult for you to be here. Is that right? I wonder if you could talk about that?' [Empathy + Form 4]. Or, 'I notice that you're looking pretty uncomfortable right now. I don't know if you feel like telling me, but I'd really be interested in being let in on what's behind that look' [Form 3].

Alternatively, we may feel that it is best not to confront the client and instead to be empathic while bringing ourselves into the picture, whereupon we might say something like:

> I'm sensing that it's a little difficult for you to be here, now that you've actually arrived. It could be that you don't know what to say, or that you don't feel safe in saying anything. I can understand how it must be difficult, coming to a stranger like this [Empathy]. I just want you to know that I feel my role here is to work *with* you in some way, if we can work out together how that might be and if, at the end of the day, you still feel interested in doing so [Form 1]. You'll probably find that as we go on today I'll not be saying much and doing a lot of listening. This will be because I believe strongly that people learn a lot about themselves by hearing themselves talk to others [Form 1]. Then, toward the end of the meeting we can talk about where to go from there [signal of eventual Form 4].

Notice that the main purposes of this metacommunication are to give defensive clients a margin of safety by indicating that they need not feel trapped in the situation; to convey some idea of what can be expected from us, and why; and to provide a glimmering about what is expected from them, and why. Notice as well that the counsellor's explanation of his or her role is far from complete. A full explanation would be confusing and overwhelming at this point. It is more prudent to give clients in this circumstance just enough of a sense of what is expected of them and involved in the situation so that they can get started. The other aspects of the counsellor's approach can be introduced and explained later on.

What about clients who *are* trapped, through coercion? In this situation, it is probably best to take the general line to the effect that the client and counsellor are 'stuck with each other' and given that that is the case, the thing to do is to try to sort out how they may make the best out of the situation, by saying something like:

> I realize that you haven't come to see me of your own free will. I don't know what you're feeling right now, but it might be something like, 'I'm mad as hell', and 'I feel so damned manipulated and powerless' [Empathy]. I just want you to know that it's not easy for me either. I'm sure you would agree that it's difficult to be of any use to a person in a situation like this unless the person is willing [Form 2, generalized to the situation]. Yet, here we are. I don't know if it helps for me to say it, but I'm interested in making something useful out of this if you are. I don't know at this point how we might

do that. All I do know is that I'm not the least interested in throwing things at you that come from where *I* stand. Instead, I'm far more interested in trying as much as possible to work from where *you're* coming from [Form 1]. Short of attacking me physically or indicating to me that you have intentions of harming others, which would force me to take steps to intervene in some way, anything you choose to do in here is fine with me [tacit Form 2 about a hypothetical situation]. I don't know if that makes much sense, but that's what I feel [tacit Form 4].

As in the last response, the counsellor begins with an empathic reach across to the client. Then follow several metacommunications tailor-made to the particular situation. They are designed to give the client a sense of control and empowerment within the counselling situation, designed to offset the fact that he or she has no control over being in the situation itself. Failure to provide this prospect of empowerment could leave the client in a state of double jeopardy. The freedom allowed is not total, however. Limits to what the client can do are imposed. Even so, paradoxically, the impartation of such limits may be freeing for the client because they may be much broader than anticipated.

Goals and tasks Clients often arrive with their own ideas of what is wrong with them and what they need. Of course, they may eventually see things otherwise as a result of their interaction with the counsellor. But, for the moment, they have an emotional investment in their current perspective and will be inclined to resist goals that differ markedly from their own preferences. Meanwhile, counsellors develop their understanding of clients' difficulties as their revelations of them unfold and gradually formulate their goals for them.

It can happen that the goals turn out to be the same. When this occurs, it remains to work out an agreement on the task(s) to be carried out to implement the goal, and then to check periodically as to whether the agreement on the goal and task(s) is intact. As much as person-centred counsellors want to ally themselves with the client's goals, it is sometimes difficult for them to quell their judgement of what is best for the client. For example, the client may be bent on salvaging a marriage with an abusive alcoholic when, from the counsellor's perspective, it seems that the spouse has no interest in rehabilitation and that the client is unduly clinging to a bad marriage. If it should happen that as counsellors we have reasons to be concerned about the safety of the client, then our desire to ally with her goal conflicts with our ethical obligation to intervene when physical danger to her is a real possibility. Even though it would complicate the counselling relationship, in this circumstance we may decide that it is necessary to lay before the client our twin goals of allying ourselves with her goal while helping her to protect herself from harm.

Such considerations notwithstanding, disjunctions between clients and counsellors more often have to do with tasks than goals. A common source of disjunction is that the client may be more in tune with desires whereas the counsellor is responding more to a sense of what the client needs. Thus, for example, clients may want to resolve their difficulties without experiencing much emotional pain, whereas the counsellor may feel that the pain must be experienced and worked through. To complicate matters, the imbalance in the power relationship between them inclines most clients to want to trust the counsellor's judgement more than their own, at least for a while. In this state, the client can spend time and energy trying to figure out just where the counsellor is coming from which, as we have seen, detracts from the client's self-focus. Meanwhile, because the client hides this kind of perplexity and instead attempts to follow the counsellor's lead, the counsellor may be given few clues about the client's inner tension – and may thus blithely carry on.

Disjunctions are serious when the client's preferred task differs dramatically from the counsellor's, as when the client wants to trace the historical roots of the trouble and the counsellor prescribes a behavioural approach; or the client wants to unearth unconscious factors while the counsellor sees the client's task as learning how to work more effectively with conscious experience; or the client sees the task as changing a troublesome partner whereas the counsellor sees it as helping the client to change herself in relation with the partner (see also Safran, Muran and Wallner Samstag, 1994). In this situation, clients may desperately try to signal to the counsellor that they do not agree with the latter's approach, through a series of 'Yes, buts' and other tacit disclaimers, short of directly challenging the counsellor. Unfortunately, the lack of explicit challenge can easily be misinterpreted by the counsellor as indicating that the client is basically content with the counsellor's approach and that the disclaimers are part of the normal negotiation that goes on when two people co-construct an understanding of a complex phenomenon.

It is better to be sceptical about clients' compliance and to check on the seeming agreement about tasks. Thus, we invite clients to share their preferred tasks and reciprocate with an indication of our own sense of the task – entering a negotiation to work out a task that is agreeable to both. Thus, in what seems like a suitable moment, we may say something like:

> Now that we have talked about it for a while, I am interested to learn of your sense of basically what's at play in the difficulty you're experiencing. I'm also interested in whether you have some idea of what the best way to proceed might be.

In person-centred counselling, the most generic conflict around tasks has to do with structure: the client may want direction whereas the counsellor feels strongly that the client needs to self-direct. Fortunately, in experiential person-centred counselling it is possible to meet such clients halfway, by virtue of the process work involved in the approach. Even so, the task that flows from this approach may have to be spelled out to clients, especially if they seek advice which has to do with the content of their experience and thus falls outside the boundary of the kind of directive work in which we are willing to engage. This orientation may take a form akin to the following:

> I can appreciate that you're feeling a little desperate right now and are anxious to get a handle on what to do [Empathy]. But I have found that it is often difficult for people to accept advice once they are given it. Instead, it seems that people get the most benefit out of having someone help them with the ways they're looking at their problems and going about solving them. Thus, I think you will find that I may be quite active at times. However, this activity will have to do with helping you to work more productively with your experience rather than giving you advice about what to do. Our goal is the same, but the way of getting there would be different [all Form 1, while the 'discuss that in any case' is a tacit Form 3 as well]. Now, I'd very much like to hear whether what I have just said makes any sense to you, and of your reaction to it [Form 4].

An explanation such as this may be sufficient to prompt the client to reply that he or she is prepared to try our way; after all, we are the experts and expertise is what the client came for. If not, then we have to see how far we can accommodate the client's wishes without unduly compromising our approach. In any event, clients' compliance with the task does not necessarily mean that they are content; they may still be restive inside while complying. Thus, it is good practice to check from time to time on the client's inner reactions to how the counselling is proceeding, and to continue the negotiation process (more on this below).

When clients find it difficult to comply with the task of counselling as proposed by the counsellor, a key to the alliance is the extent to which they *willingly* comply despite the difficulty. The philosopher Frankfurt (1971) understands the will in a way that has much to do with reflexivity and which has a direct bearing on constructive compliance. He makes a distinction between first-order and second-order desires. Thus, we may not only desire something but also may desire to desire it. First-order desires are easily undermined by competing first-order desires. Hence, for example, we may desire to quit smoking for a number of reasons – it is bad for our health, messy, politically incorrect, expensive, and so on. We may also desire not to quit because of our craving for nicotine, it gives us something to do, it is a companion, and it makes it possible to engage in cue-related behaviour like drinking coffee. A second-order desire takes into account all of these competing lower-order desires and transcends them; in this case, then, it would be a desire to desire to quit smoking. Frankfurt interprets an act of will to be behaviour that expresses a second-order desire.

Similarly, Taylor (1985) distinguishes between weak and strong evaluation. Strong evaluation is behaviour responsive to a high moral principle. Thus, when in a state of strong evaluation, we may engage in behaviour that in many respects is very painful because we have judged that it is the best thing to do.

Clients may respond to the counsellor's distinction between the client's desires and needs, and in consequence may willingly comply with the counsellor's direction regarding the task of counselling, in the sense meant by Frankfurt and Taylor. When in this state, they feel that they are in an alliance with the counsellor even though it is painful in some respects (Box 9.1). This is an ideal state of affairs for the counsellor. At the same time, it is a state that deserves deep respect; in exchange the counsellor does well to check from time to time to make sure that the pain of compliance is not pushed beyond tolerable limits. Otherwise the alliance may break down, at least temporarily.

The alliance from moment-to-moment

Thus far, we have considered the development of an agreement about goals and tasks, both during the initial meeting and beyond it. It goes without saying that goals may shift during the course of counselling and that the tasks involved correspondingly may shift along with them. Hence, a given goal and the task(s) designed to implement it need to be monitored from time to time. Apart from the importance of such monitoring, however, it is useful to remember that an alliance about goals and tasks is supported on an ongoing basis by the nature of the moment-to-moment inter-

> **Box 9.1**
> **An example of the client willingly complying with a painful counselling task**
>
> The following commentary was given by a research interviewee reflecting on complying with the task of two-chair work in gestalt therapy.
>
> *Client* OK. This is so, uh, we are getting into the past. He [i.e. the therapist] knows that I hate this part, and I know that I hate this part, but –
> *Researcher* [Interrupts] This part being what?
> *Client* When, when we start doing the two chairs, and I start acting out what I'm feeling and getting into emotions. I can't stand it. But I normally don't resist. A couple of times I will say, and will stop it. But normally I hate it and he knows I hate it but I do it anyway. I'm not really resisting. So that's what we're doing. It's just a bit of a joke that I really hate it.
>
> Reprinted from D.L. Rennie (1992) 'The client's experience of psychotherapy: the unfolding of reflexivity', in S.G. Toukmanian and D.L. Rennie (eds), *Psychotherapy Process Research: Paradigmatic and Narrative Approaches*. Newbury Park, CA: Sage. p. 222.

action between the counsellor and the client. Equally important, apart from good maintenance work, is the recognition that there is always the chance that the alliance is momentarily ruptured, and often without the counsellor's awareness, setting up the importance of repair work. Let us look at these two aspects in turn.

Maintaining the alliance Ideally, the agency at play between the client and counsellor is held in a delicate balance. As we have seen throughout the book, by virtue of the expert–client structure of the relationship, there is an asymmetrical balance of power. Yet, our meta-goal as counsellors is to have clients feel more powerful, relative to us, at the end of the counselling than they did at the beginning – we want them to draw upon our agency in such a way that they become more agential (Rennie, 1997). We do this in part by giving them jurisdiction over the content of their experience. We also do it by using process work to alert them to their agency and to help them become more effective as agents as they deal with the content of their experience. Moreover, woven throughout our process work, we make an effort to stay empathically attuned, often drawing upon our subjective experience of their experience in our attempt to connect with the leading edge of their experience.

The alliance is maintained from moment-to-moment when clients are given maximum freedom within the constraint of this expert–client relationship. This condition applies both to when we use our subjectivity when attempting to catch the leading edge of clients' experiences and to when we shift into a directive mode when working with how they are processing their experiences. Let us look at the empathic aspect and the process directive aspect in turn.

1. The empathy aspect. Although he never characterized them as such, Rogers's checking responses were Form 4 metacommunications. Correspondingly, in the present approach we check on our paraphrases and reflections, especially if there are signs coming from the client that we may be inaccurate. Doing this signals to clients that they are in the driver's seat, that we are keenly interested in them and are doing our best to understand them – all of which contribute to the maintenance of the alliance.

Checking of this sort is even more important when it comes to the impartation of images and metaphors in our attempt to catch the edge of their experience. These interventions, which may be cast in the form of evocative reflections (Rice, 1974), are often succinct and powerful. Most importantly, as much as we try to monitor the extent to which they are in tune with the leading edge of the client's experience, there is always a chance that they are inappropriate, either because they are *ahead* of the leading edge or, worse, are projections of our personal subjectivity. Hence, we give clients leeway when offering such responses when we own them, offer them tentatively and are always prepared to check on their impact. Thus, when we have an image, instead of saying, 'It's like you're in a cocoon', we say, 'You know, as you were saying that, I had an image of a cocoon. I don't know if it fits or not, but that's what came to me' [Form 2 + tacit Form 4].

2. Process work. Process work involves a deliberate shift away from the content of clients' experience to how they are working with the content. When it involves direction, we take control. When clients are stuck, they may welcome an intervention of this sort. In this situation it is perhaps less important to check with them about how they are receiving the intervention; indeed, they may non-verbally indicate that they welcome the intervention. Even so, we can remind them of how much we prize their authority if we make the shift metacommunicatively with a transition remark such as:

> I notice that you seem to have come to a halt [Process Identification]. I don't know if it would be useful or not [tacit Form 4], but one thing you could try would be to see if you can make contact with the feeling of *being* stuck [Process Direction]. That is, if you feel it might be useful [tacit Form 4].

Alternatively, clients may be highly active in their dialogue but we may judge that the activity is not especially productive. For example, the client may be storytelling from an externalized perspective, whereas we feel an internalized perspective (Toukmanian, 1986, 1992) would be more useful. At the same time, we caution ourselves that clients often tell a private story to themselves *within* the story told to the counsellor (Rennie, 1994c). If we decide in favour of interrupting, we could take all of this into account with a remark like:

> Sorry, I'm going to cut in for a moment. I notice that you're going ahead full steam right now but I can't get a sense of what you're getting at [Form 2]. It could be that as you're telling this story you're deriving significance from it for yourself that you're not letting me in on [tacit Form 3]. Or it could be that you're not [tacit Form 3]. If you are, then, please, go ahead! If you're not, then I wonder if it might not be more useful to you to derive the significance of the story *for* you [Process Direction]. What do you think? [Form 4].

A number of consequences may flow from such an intervention. At a minimum, clients are reminded that we are doing our best to understand them in our bid to help them understand themselves. This reminder in and of itself may contribute to the maintenance of the alliance. More fundamentally, the intervention could conceivably lead to a new task or even a new goal (such as learning how to be more reflective).

Repairing momentary ruptures in the alliance Even in good working alliances, there can be momentary ruptures and, because clients usually do what they can to hide them from us, they can occur without our awareness. My enquiry into the client's experience of therapy revealed many such momentary ruptures and cover-ups. For example, the counsellor who was a client (Box 4.4, p. 42) reported, elsewhere in the research interview, that she had busily and contentedly spent most of the particular hour of counselling which we focused on taking the lead in dealing with her experience. In turn, the counsellor was content for her to take the lead, reflecting as she went along. In the main, she narrated stories having to do with the previous week of work at a restaurant, where she was underemployed. Yet, at a certain point, the narrative became more painful. This was when she remembered how humiliating it had been for her to have to get down on her knees to clean chairs with vinegar. At this point, she reported to me, for the first time in the counselling session, she had wanted active support from her counsellor, in addition to his empathic listening. Her IPR report is given in Box 9.2.

Several interesting things are revealed in this account. First, the client had undergone a shift from her predominant feeling of self-support to a momentary need for support from the counsellor. Second, when he had failed to give her fully what she had needed, she had taken what was useful in his response and had blocked the rest. Third, she had experienced it distinctly as a moment of misunderstanding. Fourth, she had not mentioned the misunderstanding for fear that the counsellor would think it 'funny', by which she seems to have meant 'strange'. We can interpret this as an indication that she felt that the counsellor would feel it would have been inappropriate for her to criticize him, given the asymmetry of the relationship. Finally, she took the misunderstanding in her stride, explaining that counsellors cannot be expected to be accurate all the time.

It is possible that she hid her inner reaction so well that no counsellor could have detected it. It is also possible that there were subtle expressions of the reaction, such as a shift in gaze, a little pause and/or a shift in voice tone. When engaged in the discourse with our clients, we may notice such shifts from time to time. It is useful to remember that they could be indicators of an inner disjunction of some sort and that, if we check on the impact of our response through a Form 4 metacommunication, we may be able to remedy a momentary break in the alliance. Accordingly, enquiries such as, 'Hmm. I just noticed that you looked away as you said that (Process identification). Does that mean that what I just said does not sit well, or . . . ?' [Form 4], invite the client to move into the otherwise fearful waters of correcting our judgement, criticizing us.

It is noteworthy that the misunderstanding illustrated in Box 9.2 had occurred within a session in which the counsellor had been primarily reflective. In the present approach, changes from empathic to process work may be disjunctive when, at the moment of the shift, clients are intently engaged in a path to meaning. Accordingly, in the present approach, there is a greater need for attunement through the use of metacommunication, in comparison to literal person-centred counselling. Thus, depending on the circumstances surrounding the particular moment, we

> **Box 9.2**
> **A client's revelation of a privately experienced, momentary rupture in a good alliance**
>
> Client: There I had a feeling – it might sound strange, but it's my feeling – I had the feeling it was important that [her counsellor] said (sic) something at this point. And he said something but I think it was not exactly what I expected and then I didn't really, kind of, listen to him very much to what he says. And because it was not what I expected somehow – like, what I expected him to say was something like, Well, maybe, 'I've done a job like yours too before and I think I can relate to that. I can understand that it can be humiliating.' I think that is the kind of answer I would have –
>
> Researcher: [Interrupts] That would have hit the feeling?
>
> Client: Yup. It's not exactly what he said. He said something like more, well, you know, like, 'It's some kind of, like, temporary job to you anyway, you know.' Which did bring support a little bit but not as much. And I think I'm not willing to go and say, 'Look you didn't bring me support there.' I'm trying to get a little bit and [to] continue, and try to make him understand, you know? Like, 'No!' Well, you know [pause]
>
> Researcher: Why wouldn't you do that with him?
>
> Client: He will find it funny [English was her second language; she may have meant 'strange']. It's not important.
> It's not really important. Uh, I mean, we cannot expect a counsellor will be a hundred percent all the time. Sometimes they do bring things, sometimes they don't. Yet, I won't – if he had said the thing I mentioned before, certainly he would have fed my process much better. He didn't. Well, it's like I'm blocking him. I don't want him to interfere with my process, you know? There is one little thing, like 'The job is temporary.' That gives me support. But the other things are a little beside [the point] and I don't want to let it interfere with my process. And I think that's why it seems like we're not really communicating here.
>
> Researcher: Yes.
> Client: There's not a real understanding here.

can maintain our alliance with clients from moment-to-moment when, instead of moving directly to the process directives, we occasionally metacommunicatively bid for them (process identifications are so closely linked with empathy that they are seldom experienced as intrusive). We can use bridging statements like:

> Hmm. I wonder if it would be better for you to keep going like you are, or if we should look at how you're going about doing what you're doing [Form 3]. It's hard for me to tell [Form 2]. What's your sense? [Form 3 + tacit Form 4].

Admittedly, deciding whether or not to make a response like this puts us somewhat in a dilemma. It is possible that the client does not experience the shift to process work as intrusive, in which case the metacommunication is intrusive. Alternatively, it may be that the client is making more headway internally than we can glean from the discourse and, once we learn that through the metacommunication, we decide *not* to institute a shift to process work. It is impossible to be accurate every time in our attempt to settle the matter each time it arises. Hopefully, we learn to reduce our mistakes through trial and error. Moreover, as I have indicated from time to time throughout the book and as is exemplified in Box 9.2, clients are generally very tolerant of momentary misattunements of the alliance – even of more chronic misattunements. Nevertheless, so long as it is not overdone, metacommunicative bridging often helps to ascertain whether or not a given intervention is fitting for the client and thereby helps to either prevent a misalliance or to repair an existing one.

The alliance in the ending of the relationship

Good endings in counselling begin with good beginnings. As seen, in person-centred counselling generally, apart from the individual goals for themselves that clients set in collaboration with us, the purpose of counselling is to create a situation within which clients draw upon our agency temporarily in order to become more fully agential independently. So long as this goal is kept clearly in view throughout the course of counselling, it moves through a phase of dependency on our agency on the way to emancipation from it. Thus, it is important to monitor and to test the extent to which the emancipation has occurred, and especially when counselling is drawn to a close.

Another consideration is that learning to become more agential does not mean that clients necessarily relinquish their emotional attachment to us. It is a wonderful experience for clients to be able to trust someone to the extent that they learn to trust the counsellor, and it is often difficult for them to let go of the counselling relationship regardless of how well they are functioning. After all, even highly functioning individuals need close relationships and in today's hectic world close relationships are not all that easy to develop and maintain. Thus, throughout counselling and especially as it draws to a close, the bond involved in the working alliance needs to be taken into account as much as the extent to which the goal of counselling has been achieved.

It is important, then, for us to make sure that throughout counselling clients are monitoring their progress in terms of two key questions: 'Where am I at in terms of what I want to achieve out of counselling?', and 'Where am I am at in terms of being able to relinquish my dependency on my counsellor?' Doing this reminds clients that the counselling is meant to come to an end and that the whole point of counselling is to prepare for that ending. Naturally, once this focus is maintained, the considerations it prompts may become part of the counselling itself as when, say, the matter of dependency proves to be an *issue* and thus becomes a theme of the counselling. In any event, progress toward a constructive ending is maintained if we ask our clients from time to time, 'Where are we at now? How far along are we toward the achievement of your goal(s)? What do I mean to you presently? Could you let go of this relationship with me? If not, what will you need before you will be able to do that? What can you do to fulfil that need? Do you feel that you are actively preparing yourself *to* end this relationship?'

Provided questions such as these are kept in the forefront of the relationship, the ending may take care of itself; clients may self-monitor and through it come to know when they no longer need counselling. Alternatively, they may have to be nudged. We may feel that they are getting close to be being able to finish but they seem to be hanging on. In this situation, the challenge is to introduce the matter without giving them the impression that we are kicking them out. There is little difficulty in meeting the challenge so long as we let them know where we are coming from, with a remark such as:

> You know, as I've been thinking about you lately, I've been wondering if you're not close to getting what you have wanted to achieve out of this relationship with me. It's hard for *me* to tell, of course, but it's a sense that I've had of late. In saying this, I want you to know that I have no personal investment in the answer to the question; I'm quite content to continue so long as you feel you need it [Form 1]. I just want to open up a discussion along these lines [Form 1]. What's your sense of where you're at right now?

In response to this kind of enquiry, clients may convince us that they are not ready, in which case we carry on. Alternatively, they may indicate that they are close to feeling comfortable about ending the relationship but do not want to do it just yet. How we respond to such a reply will depend on our appraisal of the client's willingness actually to emancipate from us. A positive judgement in this respect would lead us to carry on as usual. Alternatively, should we sense that the client has come to rely on the relationship because it is comfortable, we may wish to take steps to 'wean' them from it. There are a number of ways in which this can be done.

Clients can be encouraged to dialogue with themselves or with significant others in the way they dialogue with us, independent of their meetings with us. This encouragement comes out of the recognition that, when they are away from us and encountering a difficulty, they may lazily slip into postponing dealing with it until the next counselling session. I have found that many clients can work productively with the suggestion that they carry on a dialogue with the counsellor *in their minds* when dealing with difficulties away from counselling. Apart from that technique, of course, clients can be reminded that they may have slipped into relying on the counsellor more than on friends and relatives, when the latter could be relied on instead so long as clients are prepared to make a demand on them. Depending on the client, such a reminder may have to be combined with a directive to do just that, as a homework assignment, and to report on how it went.

It is also useful to stagger the counselling sessions. Thus, for example, weekly sessions are stretched to fortnightly, then to monthly. In addition, a follow-up session at, say, six months after the final meeting can be arranged. This staggering of appointments serves the dual purpose of giving clients increasing experience in functioning on their own while still having the security of the bond. Correspondingly, gradually our importance to them recedes until the bond itself subsides.

Summary

In this chapter a number of features of experiential person-centred counselling have been drawn together and integrated with Bordin's concept of the working alliance. These elements are reflexivity; the recognition that by virtue of reflexivity both clients and counsellors operate within private worlds of experience as well as the public world of their discourse; the realization that clients are highly disposed to defer to their counsellors; the nature of the will; the finding that clients are capable of willingly complying with the expertise of the counsellor even though it is difficult and/or painful; and counsellors' use of metacommunication to reveal their purposes and the impacts of the client on them, as well as to probe for the client's purposes and the impacts of the counsellor on them. These elements are used to indicate ways in which the counsellor can facilitate the development of a working alliance irrespective of whether clients are willing at the outset to engage in counselling. They are also used to indicate how the working alliance, once initially established, may be maintained and repaired. The chapter concludes with a consideration of productive ways of ending the counselling relationship, seen as the final expression of the working alliance.

10
Training

Most of what I have to say about training is contexualized in the format of a formal *course* on it, such as the one I teach. Within such a course, it is possible to concentrate on practising being the kind of counsellor addressed in the approach. I have found that when students and their supervisors are in the throes of meeting the many demands involved in a field placement, such as a clinical practicum or an internship, it is often difficult to find the time to put case management aside to engage in extensive role-playing. Instead, training usually takes the form of listening to the replay of a tape of a given counselling session, where the trainee's approach is examined and discussed in an attempt to work out ways that the trainee might engage in more effective counselling in future meetings with his or her client.

The advantage of training in the context of case management is that it involves real counselling whereas, in a course designed around role-playing, the counselling is always artificial to a certain extent. A disadvantage of learning-while-doing, however, is that in the rush of the service work there may not be the opportunity to do the kind of work and practice that may be required to incorporate fully the main features of a given approach to counselling. In terms of the present approach, this difficulty is most evident with respect to the transition from empathic work to process work. As indicated in Chapter 7, it is often experienced as requiring emotional detachment to a certain extent, which some trainees find discomforting. (It is not always difficult, however: occasionally, a trainee encounters a client who does not respond well to empathic responding whereupon the prospect of shifting to process work is welcomed; see Box 10.1.)

Whatever the training context, I am convinced that it is best to use extensive role-playing, if possible. It can be done between a supervisor and a trainee or among members of a training group. In the first instance, the supervisor/trainer and trainee can take turns at being in the role of a client and a counsellor and can metacommunicate their conduct and experience of the roles; throughout, the supervisor guides the supervisee in the counselling approach. In the second case, more options are possible in that the trainer may act as either client, counsellor or observer.

Box 10.1
Learning process identification: motivation helps

A trainee in a clinical practicum was at her wit's end trying to deal empathically with a highly seasoned client who was sceptical about the former's youth and inexperience. She was advised to re-read the manual's chapter on process work, to replay a tape of a recent counselling session with the client and to practise substituting process identifications and directives for her customary empathic responses. In the next counselling session she used process identifications consistently, which worked. The trainee later indicated that she had learned how to do process identifications 'for life', as she put it. Thus, under the pressure of needing to come up with a different way of being with a client in order to develop the beginning of a working alliance, the student had evidently undergone one-trial learning.

In the latter situation, which is more typical of my own approach to training, my preference is to act primarily as an observer (and guide). In what follows, I begin with a consideration of role-playing, in terms of two main considerations: the first has to do with whether it is better for trainees to role-play being themselves or someone else, and the second with how the role-playing may be formatted. Note: in order to simplify the language in what follows, the terms 'client' and 'counsellor' will mean a person playing the role of a client or counsellor, as the case may be, unless specified otherwise.

Role-playing

Role-playing: who should be played?

For a number of years as a trainer I encouraged students to be themselves when being clients but I became sceptical about this approach. On the positive side, it offers the advantage of allowing counsellors to come in contact with someone with a genuine problem, so that the counsellor has 'something to work with'. Moreover, to a considerable extent, the danger that trainees may get too deeply into material can be offset when they are instructed to present a problematic aspect of experience that is not deeply personal. Nevertheless, I have concluded that the advantage of having trainees be themselves as clients is outweighed by disadvantages. As much as they may be encouraged to present only problems that are not of a serious nature, they are problems all the same and call for resolution. Also, while in the role, they and their counsellor (and everyone else in the room, especially the trainer) may discover that the problem is more serious than was thought. Either way, the trainer is pulled into being concerned for the client and, when the counsellor is floundering, the former may feel compelled to take over in order to rescue the client. Thus, the needs of the counsellor may be forsaken in order to save the client, thereby undermining the counsellor.

These negative consequences are avoided when trainees play a role. Knowing that the client is in a role, trainers do not have to worry about the client apart from paying keen attention to the experiencing communicated through the role, and can devote their full attention to the counsellor. Also, trainers have the opportunity to script particular roles to meet the needs of individual trainees. For example, if a given trainee has difficulty dealing with hostile clients, a member of the training group can be asked to be that kind of client. Best of all, I have found that provided they are given time to think about it, most trainees are marvellous in their ability to enact convincing roles. Usually this authenticity comes about because trainees play someone with whom they are familiar, such as a client that they have either counselled in the past or are counselling currently, or a friend or acquaintance. Their reports indicate that they often also empathize with their target person; when this happens, even though they are drawing upon themselves they are in a position to distance themselves from themselves because it is not *their* life that they are depicting. Overall, then, I have learned that little if any disadvantage arises from insisting that trainees role-play being clients.

Role-playing in a group situation

When training groups of students to learn individual counselling, we have to create dyadic interactions between clients and counsellors. It is up to the trainer and the group to decide the best way of doing this. One way is to have the members of the class divide themselves into pairs, with the members of each pair changing roles during a given training session or, perhaps, with pairs of dyads exchanging partners so that the counsellor in the first pair becomes the client to a counsellor in the second pair, and vice versa. The advantage of this procedure is that it maximizes the opportunity for role-playing. The disadvantage is that it dilutes the trainer's supervision because the trainer has to move from one dyad to the next, catching snatches of the discourse in each. This dilution may be reduced if the trainer has co-trainers or nominates members of the class to act as co-trainers. In the latter procedure, then, triads rather than dyads are set up, with the third member of each unit acting as an observer and trainer. This procedure does not solve the dilution problem, however, because it is highly unlikely that trainer-assistants will have the expertise of the trainer.

An alternative procedure, and the one that I have settled on, is to have a given member of the class volunteer to be the client for an entire training session (say, three hours). The remaining members of the training group take turns counselling the client and the trainer works with each trainee as his or her turn comes up. In turn, the trainees rotate being the client from session to session; it is decided at the end of a given session who will be the client in the next one and that person has the interval to prepare for the role. I have found that trainees have no difficulty being the only client for a given training session because, in the way I run a session at least, the time spent on role-playing seldom takes up more than half the class period, and often less, with the rest of the time being spent on discussion.

This approach to training thus entails a mixture of direct and vicarious learning. While the counsellor counsels the client, the trainer and the other members of the training group are present in the same room, observing. Through this observation they develop their own understanding of the client, appraise how the counselling is going and plan how they might approach it when their turn comes. Furthermore, a similar vicarious engagement occurs after their turn because, having had a turn, they are even more involved in the ensuing process and outcome.

I find that this procedure works best with a group of no more than eight trainees. With this number, the trainer has the option of initiating a single round or two rounds of counselling in an hour and a half, although I have found that it is more natural to have a single round. This gives each trainee about 10–12 minutes of counselling, which is enough for them to shift from vicarious to direct engagement.

This procedure tends to limit the practising of counselling to issues around the first counselling session because it always takes a certain amount of time for clients to explain who they are and why they have come for counselling. Upon reflection, though, I realize that this limitation may have more to do with how I run a typical course of training than with the procedure itself. In a training course of sixteen weeks (an academic term at my university), there is so much to learn regarding how to operate as a counsellor in the opening session that there is seldom a strong need to simulate later stages in counselling, especially because much of what is pertinent to the conduct of the opening session is generalizable to remaining sessions. In principle, however, there is no reason why that simulation could not be built into the client's role. Thus, it would be possible to script a role to the effect that, say, it is assumed that counselling has been going on for six months and the client does not feel that he or she is getting anywhere, or wants to focus on a new topic, or feels that the counsellor is losing interest, and so on. In the same vein, a role could be scripted where it is assumed that counselling is about to come to an end, and where the client invents a summary of the progress that was made throughout the course of counselling so that the counsellor can practise turning the working alliance into an appropriate ending.

The trainer's role

Training involves two main aspects – working with trainees in terms of their uniqueness as individuals, and guiding them in the adoption and implementation of the features of the counselling approach. Let us look at these two aspects in turn.

Working with the uniqueness of each trainee

Training people to become counsellors is rather like putting new wine into old bottles. Trainees come to a training course with their own personalities, characteristic ways of relating to people and, depending on their previous experiences, views on what constitutes good counselling. Just as in counselling itself, counsellor training involves a gradual discovery of each individual's main theme. It may have to do with attitudes toward counselling that bear on the particular approach being offered, or, more likely, with personal styles that would apply to any approach to counselling. Thus, the trainee may have a tendency either to 'mother' clients, take too much control, interpret too much, talk too much, talk too little, over-intellectualize, and so on. Paying attention to such stylistic considerations cuts along a fine line between counselling and counsellor training but is justified if the personal trait impacts significantly on the counselling approach and if, once the matter is raised, the individual trainee is willing to work on the trait with that purpose in mind.

This aspect of training is thus highly individualized, involving accommodation by both the trainer and the trainee. The trainer has to learn how to work with and prize the trainee's way of being as much as possible. In turn, the trainee is called upon to incorporate the principles of the approach to training as much as possible. Thus, trainer and trainee develop a working alliance, analogous to the alliance in the counselling relationship. The nature of this alliance determines for trainers how much they may 'push' the trainee in combating the thematic trait. Should the trainee indicate that he or she wants to be nudged, but not pushed, then the trainer has to act accordingly. Alternatively, if the trainee comes to share the trainer's concern about the trait, then the trainee may assent to strong interventions by the trainer. Thus, for example, the trainer may insist that an over-intellectualizing trainee become aware of his or her felt-sense and respond in only terms of it; may insist that an overly talkative trainee practise being silent during counselling discourse; may cajole an overly interpretive trainee into inhibiting all interpretive impulses; and so on.

Parallel to the counselling situation, once a good working alliance is developed between the trainer and individual trainee, then the trainee may take the goal of coming to grips with the personal trait firmly in hand and creatively work out his or her own solution (for an example, see Box 10.2)

> **Box 10.2**
> **One way of learning how to listen: becoming all ears**
>
> A trainee was strongly inclined to theorize and interpret too much when dialoguing with clients. He decided that he needed to listen more and talk less. He aided this decision by imagining that he had enormous ears – huge ears, like those of some sort of bat-creature. His task was now to listen with these gigantic ears. Over the course of two to three weeks, he transformed his approach dramatically and effectively.

Trainees usually find that, in working with personal themes of this sort, they have to exaggerate them at first in order to get over their inhibitory barrier. I encourage this solution, reassuring them that, once the new way of behaving is firmly in place, they will be able to relax their vigilance and move into a middle ground. I hardly need to point out the advantage of using role-playing clients when dealing with extreme shifts in response style of this sort. When concentrating on them, the attention is fully on the trainee; the client's presence is merely an occasion for the practice of alternative responding.

Training the particulars of the approach

Just as in counselling, counsellor training involves both content and process. The content consists of the main aspects of the approach. Thus in the current approach the content primarily consists of empathic responding, transparency, process work, metacommunication and the establishment of the working alliance. The process consists of the *way* in which the trainer chooses to train these contents. For example, the contents may be addressed holistically or in modules and may be taught non-directively or directively. Each trainer and training group have to work out the most satisfactory choices among these options. Nevertheless, the emphasis in the present approach on reflexivity and the unity of human experience inclines trainers to emphasize the relationship of each trainee to the contents, as a whole, of the approach. It is thus coherent with this emphasis to suggest to trainees that they should be familiar with the contents of this book in advance of beginning training, and to make an effort to implement the various practices constituting those contents, from moment-to-moment in their interaction with their clients, as seems fitting. With this intention in mind, they will find that they can either actually implement the practices, at least to some extent, or not. Unsatisfactory implementation may be noted by either the trainee or the trainer, or both, which sets the stage for collaborative activity between them.

It is always difficult for trainers to know how much they should intervene in the trainee's performances during role-playing. Performance anxiety is usually high, especially when role-playing is engaged in before the rest of the group. Meanwhile, just as is true of the client in counselling, trainees will be aware of some aspects of their beingness and less aware of others. For those aspects in awareness, they may be their own worst critics. Yet, even in that self-criticism, they learn whether or not they are willing to *do* something about whatever it is that gives rise to the criticism. And, of course, they have little chance of changing aspects of themselves about which they are unaware. It is often difficult for the trainer to tease out what is going on by virtue of these many possibilities, and to know what to do in any case. The best way to sort things out is to bring into play the four forms of metacommunication. Doing this provides a way of developing, maintaining and repairing the working alliance between the trainer and trainee. Also, having experienced alliance work in this way, it is easier for the trainee to apply these same principles when in the role of the counsellor.

Mixed up in all of this is the matter of flow. Trainees have their own tacit goals that they find themselves developing as they interact with clients; they also work out their own strategies to reach the goals. There is more than one road to Rome. Also, in the round robin approach to dyadic work that I am addressing, each trainee has only about ten minutes available and it takes a few moments to get into a flow. All of these considerations make trainers hesitate before intervening in the interaction between trainee and client. Yet, if the flow is allowed to go on too long, the trainee may be denied constructive criticism. This balance between silent observation and active intervention has to be worked out for each trainee. Having said that, I have found that most trainees prefer the trainer to intervene. It is then left for the trainer to decide how much intervention can occur without it being too disruptive.

I find that the contents divide naturally into four main categories: empathic work, transparency and metacommunication, process identification and direction, and the working alliance. Each involves challenges.

Training in empathic work: finding the edge Especially when they start to learn how to counsel, trainees have difficulty avoiding spotty listening and thus often miss the leading edge of the client's experience. Spotty listening is promoted by trainees' appraisals of how they are performing – which, as indicated, is made worse by being observed. Meanwhile, the trainer is more secure and not in the hot seat, and is thus better able to listen keenly to the client and to respond to his or her (the trainer's) felt-sense of the client's felt-sense. When there are disparities between the trainer's sense of the leading edge and where the trainee is going in the discourse, then the trainer may wish to intervene. Sometimes the intervention makes perfect sense to the trainee once it is drawn to his or her attention. Usually, in this circumstance, the trainee has had a tacit sense of the edge but either could not bring it sufficiently into awareness or did not know how to address it. In this situation, the best course of action is to give the trainee the lead in working out a way of expressing his or her felt-sense of the edge, refining the response if it seems appropriate. Alternatively, the trainee may have a different sense of the edge. If this is the case, it has to be negotiated because, after all, the trainer could be wrong (appealing to the client or, perhaps, to the other members of the group is helpful in determining who is closer to the mark – the trainee or trainer; when taking this initiative, it is important to try to defuse the client's and/or the group's deference to the trainer). Typical work with trainees regarding responding in terms of the leading edge of the client's experience is illustrated in Box 10.3 where the opening discourse between a trainee and a client is reported and, midway through it, the trainer intervened.

Transparency and metacommunication Although good empathic responding involves the counsellor's use of his or her internal experience, that experience is used to facilitate focus on the client's experience. Hence, the personal experience of the counsellor is mediated through the experience of the other person, which protects counsellors from having to reveal themselves. Transparency and metacommunication are different. In this way of relating, the counsellor is more exposed; trainees often feel anxious when faced with the prospect of communicating in this way and are more resistant. Nevertheless, if they can be encouraged to break through that barrier, they are open to the richness provided by these alternative ways of discoursing.

Teaching trainees to learn to feel comfortable working with their inner experience – when it involves uncertainties, insecurities and doubts – entails both theory and practice. The ontology supporting the current approach to counselling needs to be appealed to time and again. This is not to say that trainees should be brainwashed, but it is important for them to be able realize deeply and emotionally the full significance of the ontology. At the same time, it is equally important not to stray too far in the direction of theory and away from practice; it is up to each trainer and training group to work out an appropriate balance.

The atmosphere within the training group is critically important. Trainees are more willing to risk exposure when they feel that the group situation is safe. It is up to the trainer to set the tone for a trusting atmosphere by being supportive, never belittling. The line between a therapy group and a task-group can get a little fine at times; because the trainer wants to be sensitive to every trainee's needs, it can sometimes happen that the trainer gets pulled by the personal needs of given trainees that envelop and exceed the training task. It is difficult to avoid these imbalances at

> **Box 10.3**
> **The opening discourse between a trainee and a client**
>
> **Trainee** Hi, I'm Jane and I'm a graduate student in psychology. And you are [pause]?
> **Client** Hi, I'm Lara. I don't know how much you know about me. I called and I just wanted to come in to talk to somebody.
> **Trainee** What would you like to talk about?
> **Client** It's funny. I had so much on my mind all the way here! And now I'm not sure what to say. [12 seconds' pause] It's just, uh, [pause] I'm going through a really difficult time right now. Uh, I split up with my husband [sighs] a couple of months ago. And, uh, I'm stressed out as you can probably tell [sharp expiration of breath]. There's just been a lot of things going on. At home, with me and my 10-year-old son.
> **Trainee** Since the separation?
> **Client** Yeah. Well, things have built up. I just don't have [explosive sigh] – the same patience that I, that I had.
> **Trainee** Patience with your son?
> **Client** [25 seconds' pause, at which point the trainer intervenes]
> **Trainer** What's the edge here?
> **Trainee** I think it's the issue with her son.
> **Trainer** What's the edge?
> [Someone else in the training group says something that is unclear on the tape]
> **Trainer** Yes, it's hard to talk about. She started talking about it, but she stopped when she got to her son. Right? This is the edge. It's hard to talk about. This is where it's difficult, see? She's not giving us the edge by what she's saying; she's now giving us the edge by what she's doing. She's stopped talking. OK? So, then, your response is, 'It's hard to talk about.'
> [The trainee says to the client, 'It's hard to talk about', and continues the dialogue.]

times but occasional metacommunicative dialogues about how the training is going are helpful.

Within an accepting group atmosphere, trainees may be nudged into being transparent and metacommunicative. The timing is important. It is natural for people to do something aversive if it is less aversive than what they are currently experiencing; putting it another way, when feeling that they have nothing to lose, trainees are more willing to try anything. Thus, when in desperation the trainee breaks out of role and turns to the trainer with, 'I'm stuck. I don't know where to go from here', the trainer can smoothly suggest, 'Why don't you say that to the client?' In the same vein, when the trainer senses that the trainee is getting bogged down, the former can ask, 'What are you experiencing right now? Perhaps you have had an image of some sort, or are sitting on a metaphor – something imaginative.' If the trainer's hunch is correct, then the trainee can be encouraged to communicate it to the client – and metacommunicatively as well. Box 10.4 contains an example of the typical discussion that goes on between the trainer and members of the training group when the former encourages metacommunication and transparency.

Box 10.4
Some discussion about metacommunication and transparency

The following interaction between a trainer and a trainee occurred in the context of the counselling of a (role-playing) client who was concerned about her relations at work. She had brought into the counselling a note from her work supervisor, which none of the trainees who had taken a turn at counselling her had read, even though the client had three times subtly invited the various counsellors to do so. At the point at which the following discussion began, there was consideration about the awkwardness around the reading of the note. The trainer used the occasion to address metacommunication, and then transparency.

Trainer	Now, the other way that one can use the awkwardness to advantage is to move into a sort of interpersonal therapy mode where you're taking note of what's going on between you and her, and that she's appealing to your judgement about the note, which of course is an indication that she doesn't trust her own judgement about notes.
Trainee	Right.
Trainer	And so we can make an identification to her that seems to be what's going on here, and get her to reflect on whether that is sort of typical of what she's going through these days. And then that throws her back on herself but in a way that is deeply integral to what's going on in the moment between the two of you. And, and, and then, it takes you out of being awkward and back into being productive with her.

Trainee	Mmm hmm. I think I tried to do that a bit earlier where I said, 'You're not able even trust your judgement, your feelings', because she was she was kind of saying this, but at the same time I found myself thinking that she seems so sensitive – she explored about this, this note and then immediately went into another situation with the boss, that I'm thinking, 'She's so *sensitive*, how am I going to get this alliance [laughs ruefully] – with this woman?', and I kept feeling that I wanted to say, 'Can you just slow down?', and you know, sort of [snaps fingers] – but I didn't find the time to
Trainer	[Interrupts] Well, these are all inner thoughts that maybe you could benefit from. You see, it might have been useful for you to say that to her.
Trainee	To her, yeah. I kept looking for places to – but I didn't want – again, I didn't want – I think I was hearing, you know, 'Beginning counsellors try to talk too much! It's OK to let clients go.' So, I thought, 'Just let her go. She's going to run out of' [hesitates, laughs].
Trainer	Yeah. I guess all I'm saying is that, uh, especially because we're role-playing in this class – every time you're up in that chair, you're into an experimental situation. You're not into a genuine sort of therapeutic situation, you're into an experiment. And, it gives you much more flexibility to experiment, to try things, you know, which are in keeping with the things we are talking about in the class – even though they would not necessarily be the kind of things you would want to do if this were a real counselling situation. It's a way of giving yourselves an opportunity to stretch behaviourally as counsellors. [One of the themes of the approach] is that it's OK to work as productively as possible with one's internal experience of the moment-to-moment interaction with the client. So, if you're feeling something, you can experiment with sharing that feeling.
Trainee	Yeah.
Trainer	It could not work out, but at least you'll have the experience of getting those words out.
Trainee	Sure. And her feedback about what that was like.

When well timed, interventions like the one reported in Box 10.4 encourage trainees to draw genuinely on their inner experience and, once they are over the hurdle, they are usually rewarded for it. It is internally rewarding because it helps to diminish the tension that was associated with being stuck; it feels good to be able to be real with the client and to let oneself off the hook. It also contributes to the working alliance, which is doubly rewarding.

Process identification and process direction   As addressed in Chapter 7, shifting from empathic to process responding involves a kind of detachment that can be uncomfortable for trainees because they fear that they are losing contact with the client and may feel somewhat guilty. It is thus important for them to experience as early as possible in training, when in the role of the client, having a counsellor use process responses. This experience often reduces biases against them. Even when comfortable with the idea of using them, however, actually doing so is still difficult for some trainees. They now have to be prepared to act on more awareness – of body language and voice tone as well as the meanings of words. 'When do you do what?', they wonder.

Ideally, process work becomes another language that the counsellor can slip into at will depending on the contingency of the moment with the client. Achieving fluency can be reached artificially, naturally, or by a mixture of the two. The artificial approach is to insist that a given trainee give nothing but process responses during the course of a dialogue with a client for, say, five minutes at a time. This technique is cast an experiment, which ethically can be done because, once again, the counselling is directed toward a role-playing client who, for that matter, can be asked what it was like to addressed in this way. Alternatively, in the natural way, trainees are reminded of process work, and of what it entails, at the outset of discourse with the client and are encouraged to shift to a process mode when it seems appropriate. As a guide to such shifts, they are encouraged to be in tune with their felt-sense of the client's felt-sense and, when it seems like a process response might be more useful than an empathic response in a given moment, to try it. They may also be encouraged to probe metacommunicatively for its impact and to integrate the reply into the working alliance, if it seems appropriate. Between these two alternatives, the trainer may seize upon an opportunity from time to time to make an intervention. An example of the latter approach is given in Box 10.5.

Trainees generally find it easier to make process identifications than process directives. The former are less disruptive; they are confluent with the client's path. The latter are qualitatively different in that they involve a judgement that the client may be better off doing something other than what he or she is doing, or by doing it differently. This manoeuvre is a clear-cut assumption of power and taking it makes many trainees squirm. The bridge to

> **Box 10.5**
> **An example of training in process identification**
>
> The following excerpt is drawn from a training session midway through a 16-week programme of three-hour weekly training sessions. The client had been dealing with mistrust of her husband and had indicated that she needed a guarantee from him. At the same time, she had indicated, she did not need a guarantee in other aspects of her life, only this one. The trainer took this realization as an opportunity to encourage the trainee to use a process identification.
>
> | | |
> |---|---|
> | Trainer | OK. Just as an exercise, this is an opportunity to do a little bit of process work because what she has done here is very interesting, which is that she recognizes that she doesn't need guarantees in all sectors of her life. |
> | Trainee | Mmm hmm. |
> | Trainer | It's just in *this* one. |
> | Trainee | Mmm hmm. |
> | Trainer | And you might draw her attention to that, so that she can begin to – sort of – work with that differentiation. |
> | Trainee | [Turns to the client] So, what is it about this part of your life – |
> | Trainer | [Interrupts] But, just for the exercise, put it into a process identification. |
> | Trainee | [Turns to client] So you, so you've said that, in terms of your marriage, you need a guarantee but, at the same time you're saying that, in other parts of your life, you know that there are no guarantees, and you don't need them. |
> | Trainer | That's better, but I wouldn't use, 'said'. I would use, 'recognize'. 'You recognize that you don't need guarantees in *other* sectors of your life except for this one, which is different.' *Say* it! [General laughter] Just for the practice. |
> | Trainee | Do it the way you say it [laughs]. OK. [Turns to client] OK. You've *recognized* that in other parts of your life that you don't need a guarantee, but this is different. |

this kind of responding is to remind trainees that this is where metacommunication is especially helpful. It may be emphasized that the process directive can be made tentatively, offered as an experiment, and checked for its impact. All of the returns from such metacommunications may be translated into a working alliance and, once that is established, trainees need no longer feel so guilty about being directive. Once again, the virtue of training in a role-playing environment is evident. Trainees are encouraged by the realization that the impact of their interventions does not fall on a person in genuine distress. At the same time, there is considerable ecological validity in the role-playing client's feedback on the impact of the interventions, such that the trainee may justifiably feel confident in applying them with real clients, so long as the directives are accompanied by the appropriate checks.

Box 10.6 illustrates a typical intervention by the trainer, designed to teach how to move into process direction. When we look at the trainee's response to the trainer's suggestion, we see that she used passive language. The trainer suggested that she say, 'Maybe you should think . . . ', which was a bid for an active process directive moderated by tentativeness. The trainee translated this suggestion into, 'If you think about it, what do you think it is . . . ', which was a passive process directive sharpened by a request for an answer. Thus, the trainee avoided taking the full plunge into a process directive. She had made an effort, however, and the trainer decided to reward the effort by not pushing further. Depending on the trainee, and the circumstances, he could have chosen to point out the disparity and have the trainee try again.

Training with respect to the working alliance   Last but not least is the matter of teaching students to pay attention to the working alliance. Beginning counsellors, and especially those working within the person-centred framework however broadly defined it may be, are prone to give insufficient consideration to what it is, overall, that they and the client are doing together. They easily lull themselves into believing that empathic work is inherently healing and that clients will doubtless come back for more – that the alliance naturally takes care of itself. Although this complacency may be justified, it is often difficult to know just *what* the client is experiencing. Consequently, the best way to learn is to check, and frequently. Thus, in training, it is useful to remind trainees that they and the client will benefit if they monitor their sense of how well a given session is going – especially the opening session – and, if they sense that it is not going well, to check with the client (metacommunication, Form 4). Done early enough in an opening session, the feedback may enable the counsellor to change direction in order to save the session; done early enough in an ongoing relationship, it may enhance the alliance.

Box 10.6
An example of training in process direction

This example is drawn from the dialogue with the same 'client' addressed in Box 10.5. The counselling had moved further along, and a different trainee had assumed the role of counsellor. At this point, the client talked about control. The trainee carried on from where the last counsellor had left off with the following opening query. Later, the trainer intervened, as will be seen.

Trainee   Claire, do you think that maintaining control in the sense of having a choice as to whether to confront your husband or not, is that retaining control for you?

Client   Well, yeah, I hadn't thought of it in that framework but it's starting to make sense to me. I hear myself asking for a guarantee, and I hear myself, you know, controlling when I don't say anything, so it would be impossible for me to ignore that.

Trainee   Mmm hmm.

Client   But, knowing that, having that insight doesn't help me in terms of knowing what to do or [pause]

Trainee   Mmm hmm. Mmm hmm.

Client   Because I don't how I'm trying to control. I don't know if I'm trying to control him, his life, what he's been up to or whether I'm trying to control my own feelings, or my own view of my, my marriage. Or my own investment in my marriage. I don't know what I'm trying to control or hold on to.

Trainee   Mmm hmm. You're not sure what you're trying to hold on to. What are you holding on to? [At this point the trainer intervened.]

Trainer   Not quite. You don't want to rub her nose too much in what she's just said she can't do.

Trainee   Uh huh.

Trainer   Uh, nor do you want to let it go.

Trainee   Right.

Trainer   Uhm, you might put it this way. 'Right. It *is* difficult. But it also sounds very important. Maybe you should think about it – What is it, you know, *about* what it is that you're trying to control?' Just, keep her on the spot.

Trainee   Uh huh. I didn't mean to, uh, [laughs with a little embarrassment]. [Turns to client] It is, it *is* difficult – right. If you think about it, what do you think it is that you're trying to control. What *might* it be?

Client   [Responded that she didn't know, then reflected that she experienced a lot of fear, which she related to a fear of change of any sort, i.e. she deepened her exploration.]

As seen in the last chapter, a major theme of the current approach is that the concept of the alliance ties together the ingredients of the present approach to counselling. Thus trainees are encouraged to consider what they and the client are doing, in any given moment, in terms of its implications for the alliance because the alliance is involved in every moment, whether the members of the dyad are fully aware of the fact or not. In turn, they are encouraged to draw upon their full resources, amplified by the principles outlined in the book and by training programmes flowing from it, in bringing the promise of experiential person-centred counselling to fulfilment.

Summary

When considering training, I have suggested that many of the ways of being addressed in the book are enhanced perhaps most effectively by role-playing in a training group. I have developed this belief after working for a number of years as a trainer in the approach and have come to realize that, like all approaches to the training of therapeutic practitioners, trainees have to give up certain ways of being in exchange for others. Also it is useful to be able to practise the exchange in a safe learning environment. At the same time, I have indicated that training can be integrated into case management so long as the supervisor is proficient at implementing many of the ingredients of the present approach, or at least is sympathetic to them, and takes time out from case management to engage in some role-playing, as needed. Finally, it is conceivable that a counsellor working in the field, and with little supervision, could use this text as a self-help book and find benefit from it – especially when pressed, in a way analogous to the trainee mentioned in the chapter who, when in a clinical practicum, was severely challenged by a confronting client. When working solo with the book, one way to proceed would be to engage in imaginative variation of customary ways of being with clients together with the ways outlined in the book, and to support this imaginative work with the replaying of tapes of sessions with clients in which the new way of responding is practised. Rehearsals of this sort should facilitate adoption of the approach.

11
Conclusion

I was at a conference recently and discussed the concept of reflexivity with a colleague who was familiar with the literature on Eastern thought. He was sceptical about reflexivity as an aid to functioning, maintaining that the state of being *in flow* is superior. The examples he gave had primarily to do with athletics, but I take his point more generally. I am reminded of Rogers's remark at the end of counselling Gloria in the 'Gloria' film, to the effect that he did not remember very much of what went on in the session because he was so immersed in the client's experience, and he considered that to be a sign that the session had probably gone well. I too have had such moments as a counsellor and, indeed, there are times when the client and I seem deeply connected. In them I do not think about what I am about to say, but just say it – my responses are intentions-in-action.

Perhaps this state of non-reflexive communication is the ideal toward which we should all strive. The approach outlined in this book is not offered as a disputation of that ideal. Instead, it is meant to close the gap between the extreme, counter-productive reflexivity that besieges beginning counsellors and the ideal of creative, empathic flow. It is also meant to point out that clients, as well, are often not in flow and to offer a guide on how to respond to them effectively when they are in that state. After all, it is when we free ourselves to work productively with the disjunctions within ourselves and within our clients – disjunctions come into awareness through reflexivity – that we pave the way to flow.

References

Alcorn, L. and Rennie, D.L. (1981) 'A comparative analysis of verbal helping responses of counselors, nurses, salespersons and teachers', *American Journal of Community Psychology*, 8: 617–20.

Angus, L.E. and Rennie, D.L. (1988) 'Therapist participation in metaphor generation: Collaborative and noncollaborative styles', *Psychotherapy*, 25: 552–60.

Angus, L.E. and Rennie, D.L. (1989) 'Envisioning the representation world: The client's experience of metaphoric expressive in psychotherapy', *Psychotherapy*, 26: 373–9.

Bohart, A. (1997) 'The client as an active self-healer: The conceptualizing-exploring experiencing process', in A. Bohart (Chair), *The Client's Active Role in Change: Implications for Integration*, symposium presented at the annual meeting of the Society for the Exploration of Psychotherapy Integration, Toronto.

Bohart, A. and Tallman, K. (1996) 'The active client: Therapy as self-help', *Journal of Humanistic Psychology*, 36: 7–30.

Bordin, E. (1979) 'The generalizability of the psychoanalytic concept of the working alliance', *Psychotherapy: Theory, Research and Practice*, 16: 252–60.

Bozarth, J.D. (1984) 'Beyond reflection: Emergent modes of empathy', in J. Levant and J. Schlein (eds), *Client-Centered Therapy and the Person-Centered Approach: New Directions in Theory, Research and Practice*. New York: Praeger. pp. 59–75.

Bozarth, J.D. (1990a) 'The essence of client-centered therapy', in G. Lietaer, J. Rombauts and R. Van Balen (eds), *Client-Centered and Experiential Psychotherapy in the Nineties*. Leuven: Leuven University Press. pp. 59–64.

Bozarth, J.D. (1990b) 'The evolution of Carl Rogers as a therapist', *Person-Centered Review*, 4: 387–93.

Braaten, L.J. (1986) 'Thirty years with Rogers's necessary and sufficient conditions of therapeutic personality change', *Person-Centered Review*, 1: 37–49.

Bozarth, J.D. and Brodley, B.T. (1986) 'Client-centered psychotherapy: A statement', *Person-Centered Review*, 1: 262–71.

Brodley, B.T. (1990) 'Client-centered and experiential: Two different therapies', in G. Lietaer, J. Rombauts and R. Van Balen (eds), *Client-Centered and Experiential Psychotherapy in the Nineties*. Leuven: Leuven University Press. pp. 87–108.

Bucci, W. (1985) 'Dual coding: A cognitive model for psychoanalytic research', *Journal of the American Psychoanalytic Association*, 3: 571–607.

Butler, J.M. and Rice, L.N. (1963) 'Adience, self-actualization, and drive theory', in J. Wepman and R. Heine (eds), *Concepts of Personality*. Chicago: Aldine. pp. 79–110.

Carkhuff, R.R. (1969) *Helping and Human Relations*, Vol. 1. New York: Holt, Rinehart and Winston.

Donald, M. (1991) *Origins of the Modern Mind: Three Stages in the Evolution of Culture and Cognition*. Cambridge, MA: Harvard University Press.

Elliott, R. (1986) 'Interpersonal Process Recall (IPR) as a process research method',

References

in L.S. Greenberg and W. Pinsof (eds), *The Psychotherapeutic Process: A Research Handbook*. New York: Guilford. pp. 503–27.

Elliott, R., James, E., Reimschuessel, C., Cislo, D. and Sack, N. (1985) 'Significant events and the analysis of immediate therapeutic impacts', *Psychotherapy*, 22: 620–30.

Ford, J.G. (1991) 'Rogerian self-actualization. A clarification of meaning', *Journal of Humanistic Psychology*, 31: 101–11.

Frankfurt, H.G. (1971) 'The freedom of the will and the concept of a person', *The Journal of Philosophy*, 68: 5–20.

Freud, S. (1958) 'The dynamics of the transference', in J. Strachey (ed. and trans.), *The Standard Edition of the Complete Psychological Works of Sigmund Freud* (Vol. 12, pp. 99–108). London: Hogarth Press. First published in 1912.

Gendlin, E.T. (1962) *Experiencing and the Creation of Meaning*. New York: Free Press.

Gendlin, E.T. (1974) 'Client-centered and experiential psychotherapy', in D.A. Wexler and L.N. Rice (eds), *Innovations in Client-Centered Therapy*. New York: Wiley. pp. 211–46.

Gendlin, E.T. (1978/1979) '*Befindlichkeit*: Heidegger and the philosophy of psychology', *Review of Existential Psychology and Psychiatry*, 16: 43–71.

Gendlin, E.T. (1981) *Focusing*, second edition. New York: Bantam Books.

Gendlin, E.T. (1990) 'The small steps of the therapy process: How they come and how we help them come', in G. Lietaer, R. Rombauts and R. Van Balen (eds), *Client-Centered and Experiential Therapy in the Nineties*. Leuven: Leuven University Press. pp. 205–24.

Gendlin, E.T. (1996) *Focusing-Oriented Psychotherapy: A Manual of the Experiential Method*. New York: Guilford.

Greenberg, L.S. (1984) 'A task analysis of intrapersonal conflict resolution', in L.N. Rice and L.S. Greenberg (eds), *Patterns of Change: Intensive Analysis of Psychotherapeutic Process*. New York: Guilford. pp. 67–123.

Greenberg, L.S., Rice, L.N. and Elliott, R. (1993) *Facilitating Emotional Change: A Moment-by-Moment Process*. New York: Guilford.

Greenson, R. (1967) *The Technique and Practice of Psychoanalysis*. Madison, CT: International Universities Press.

Habermas, J. (1971) *Knowledge and Human Interests* (Jeremy Shapiro, trans.). Boston: Beacon Press. First published in 1968.

Hill, C.E., Thompson, G.J., Cogar, M.C. and Denman, D.W. III (1993) 'Beneath the surface of long-term memory: Therapists and clients report on their own and each other's covert process', *Journal of Counseling Psychology*, 40: 278–87.

Holdstock, L.T. (1996) 'Discrepancy between the person-centered theories of self and of therapy', in R. Hutterer, G. Pawlowsky, P.F. Schmid and R. Stipsits (eds), *Client-Centered and Experiential Psychotherapy: A Paradigm in Motion*. Frankfurt am Main: Peter Lang. pp. 47–52.

Horvath, A.O. (1994) 'Empirical validation of Bordin's pantheoretical model of the alliance: The Working Alliance Inventory Perspective', in A.O. Horvath and L.S. Greenberg (eds), *The Working Alliance: Theory, Research, and Practice*. New York: Wiley. pp. 109–30.

Horvath, A.O. and Greenberg, L.S. (1994) 'Introduction', in A.O. Horvath and L.S. Greenberg (eds), *The Working Alliance: Theory, Research, and Practice*. New York: Wiley. pp. 1–12.

Ivey, A.E. (1971) *Microcounseling: Innovations in Interviewer Training*. Springfield, IL: Thomas.
Ivey, A.E. and Simek-Downing, L. (1980) *Counseling and Psychotherapy: Skills, Theory and Practice*. Toronto: Prentice-Hall.
James, W. (1950) *The Principles of Psychology*, Vol. 1. New York: Dover. First published in 1890.
Kagan, N. (1975) *Interpersonal Process Recall: A Method for Influencing Human Interaction*. (Available from N. Kagan, Educational Psychology Department, University Park, Houston, TX, 77004.)
Kiesler, D.J. (1982) 'Confronting the client–therapist relationship in psychotherapy', in J.C. Anchin and D.J. Kiesler (eds), *Handbook of Interpersonal Psychotherapy*. Elmsford, NY: Pergamon. pp. 274–95.
Kiesler, D.J. (1996) *Contemporary Interpersonal Theory and Research: Personality, Psychopathology, and Psychotherapy*. New York: Wiley.
Laing, R.D. (1967) *The Politics of Experience*. New York: Ballantine.
Land, D. (1996) 'Partial view', in R. Hutterer, G. Pawlowsky, P.F. Schmid and R. Stipsits (eds), *Client-Centered and Experiential Psychotherapy: A Paradigm in Motion*. Frankfurt am Main: Peter Lang. pp. 67–74.
Leary, T.F. (1957) *Interpersonal Diagnosis of Personality*. New York: Ronald.
Liesjssen, M. (1990) 'On focusing and the necessary conditions of therapeutic personality change', in G. Lietaer, J. Rombauts and R. Van Balen (eds), *Client-Centered and Experiential Psychotherapy in the Nineties*. Leuven: Leuven University Press. pp. 225–50.
Lietaer, G. (1984) 'Unconditional positive regard: A controversial basic attitude in client-centered therapy', in R.F. Levant and J.M. Shlien (eds), *Client-Centered Therapy and the Person-Centered Approach: New Directions in Theory, Research and Practice*. New York: Praeger. pp. 41–58. (Translated from G. Lietaer, 'Onvoorwaadelikjke Aanvaading Een Omstreden Grondhouding in Client-Centered Therapie', in *Gedrage, Dynamische Relatie en Bete Keniswereld*. Liber Amicorum Prof. J.R. Nuttin. Leuvense University Pers, 1980. pp. 145–59.)
Lietaer, G. (1989) Contribution to D.J. Cain (ed.), 'Proposals for the future of client-centered and experiential psychotherapy', *Person-Centered Review*, 4: 11–26.
Luborsky, L. (1994) 'Therapeutic alliances as predictors of psychotherapy outcomes: Factors explaining predictive success', in A.O. Horvath and L.S. Greenberg (eds), *The Working Alliance: Theory, Research, and Practice*. New York: Wiley. pp. 38–50.
Macmurray, J. (1957) *The Self as Agent*. New York: Harpers.
Maddi, S.R. (1988) 'On the problem of accepting facticity and pursuing possibility', in S.B. Messer, L.A. Sass and R.L. Woolfolk (eds), *Hermeneutics and Psychological Theory: Interpretation Perspectives on Personality, Psychotherapy, and Psychopathology*. New Brunswick: Rutgers University Press.
Margolis, J. (1986) *The Persistence of Reality 1: Pragmatism without Foundations: Reconciling Realism and Relativism*. Oxford and New York: Basil Blackwell.
Margolis, J. (1987) *The Persistence of Reality 2: Science Without Unity: Reconciling the Human and Natural Sciences*. Oxford and New York: Basil Blackwell.
May, R. (1958a) 'The origins and significance of the existential movement in psychology', in R. May, R. Angel and H.R. Ellenberger (eds), *Existence: A New Dimension in Psychiatry and Psychology*. New York: Basic Books. pp. 3–36.
May, R. (1958b) 'Contributions of existential psychiatry', in R. May, R. Angel and

References

H.R. Ellenberger (eds), *Existence: A New Dimension in Psychiatry and Psychology.* New York: Basic Books. pp. 38–92.

May, R., Angel, R. and Ellenberger, H.R. (eds) (1958) *Existence: A New Dimension in Psychiatry and Psychology.* New York: Basic Books.

McLeod, J. (1993) *An Introduction to Counselling.* Buckingham: Open University Press.

Mead, G.H. (1934) *Mind, Self, and Society.* Chicago, IL: University of Chicago Press.

Mearns, D. (1994) *Developing Person-Centred Counselling.* London: Sage.

Mearns, D. and Thorne, B. (1988) *Person-Centred Counselling in Action.* London: Sage.

Merleau-Ponty, M. (1962) *Phenomenology of Perception* (Colin Smith, trans.). London and New York: Routledge.

Miller, L.A. (1972) 'Resource-centered counselor–client interaction in rehabilitation settings', in J.D. Bozarth (ed.), *Models and functions of Counseling for Applied Settings and Rehabilitation Workers*, second edition. Hot Springs: University of Arkansas Press. (Cited in Bozarth, J.D. [1990] 'The evolution of Carl Rogers as a Therapist', *Person-Centered Review*, 4: 387–93.)

Murphy, A.E. (1951) 'Dewey's epistemology and metaphysics', in P.A. Schilpp (ed.), *The Philosophy of John Dewey*, second edition. New York: Tudor. pp. 193–235.

Noble, S. (1986) *Comfort: The Psychotherapy Client's Bottom Line.* Unpublished Honours BA thesis, Department of Psychology, York University, North York, Ontario, M3J 1P3.

O'Hara, M.M. (1984) 'Person-centered gestalt: Toward a holistic synthesis', in R. F. Levant and J.M. Shlien (eds), *Client-Centered Therapy and the Person-Centered Approach: New Directions in Therapy Theory, Research and Practice.* New York: Praeger. pp. 222–42.

O'Hara, M.M. (1995) 'Streams: On becoming a postmodern person', in M. Suhd (ed.), *Positive Regard: Carl Rogers and Other Notables He Influenced.* Palo Alto, CA: Science and Behavior Books.

Paivio, A. (1986) *Mental Representations: A Dual-Coding Approach.* London: Oxford University Press.

Patterson, C.H. (1990) 'On being client-centered', *Person-Centered Review*, 4: 425–32.

Pearson, P.H. (1974) 'Conceptualizing and measuring openness to experience in the context of psychotherapy', in D.A. Wexler and L.N. Rice (eds), *Innovations in Client-Centered Therapy.* New York: Wiley. pp. 139–70.

Phillips, J.R. (1984) 'Influences on personal growth as viewed by former psychotherapy patients', *Dissertation Abstracts International*, 46: 2820B.

Phillips, J.R. (1985) 'Influences on personal growth as viewed by former psychotherapy patients', in D.L. Rennie (Chair), *The Phenomenological Experience of Psychotherapy Treatment*, symposium presented at the annual meeting of the Human Science Research Conference, Edmonton, Alberta, Canada.

Quartaro, G.K. and Rennie, D.L. (1983) 'Effects of trainee expectancies and specific instructions on counseling skill acquisition', *Canadian Journal of Behavioural Science*, 15: 174–5.

Rennie, D.L. (1984) 'Client's tape-assisted recall of psychotherapy: A qualitative analysis', in D.L. Rennie (Chair), *Recent Advances in Psychotherapy Research: The*

Experience of the Client, symposium presented at the annual meeting of the Canadian Psychological Association, Ottawa.

Rennie, D.L. (1990) 'Toward a representation of the client's experience of the psychotherapy hour', in G. Lietaer, J. Rombauts and R. Van Balen (eds), *Client-Centered and Experiential Psychotherapy in the Nineties.* Leuven: Leuven University Press. pp. 155–72.

Rennie, D.L. (1992) 'Qualitative analysis of the client's experience of psychotherapy: The unfolding of reflexivity', in S.G. Toukmanian and D.L. Rennie (eds), *Psychotherapy Process Research: Paradigmatic and Narrative Approaches.* Newbury Park, CA: Sage. pp. 211–33.

Rennie, D.L. (1994a) 'Clients' deference in psychotherapy', *Journal of Counseling Psychology,* 41: 427–37.

Rennie, D.L. (1994b) 'Clients' accounts of resistance: A qualitative analysis', *Canadian Journal of Counselling,* 28: 43–57.

Rennie, D.L. (1994c) 'Storytelling in psychotherapy: The client's subjective experience', *Psychotherapy,* 31: 234–43.

Rennie, D.L. (1995) 'Strategic choices in a qualitative approach to psychotherapy research', in L. Hoshmand and J. Martin (eds), *Research as Praxis: Lessons from Programmatic Research in Therapeutic Psychology.* New York: Teachers College Press. pp. 198–220.

Rennie, D.L. (1996) 'Fifteen years of doing qualitative psychotherapy process research', *British Journal of Guidance and Counselling,* 24: 317–27

Rennie, D.L. (1997) 'Aspects of the client's conscious control of the psychotherapeutic process', in A. Bohart (Chair), *The Clients Active Role in Change: Implications for Integration,* symposium presented at the annual meeting of the Society for the Exploration of Psychotherapy Integration, Toronto.

Rennie, D.L. (1998) 'Grounded theory methodology: The pressing need for a coherent logic of justification', *Theory & Psychology,* 8: 101–19.

Rennie, D.L., Burke, H. and Toukmanian, S.G. (1978) 'Counsellor communication style as a determinant of rater-perceived empathy', *Canadian Counsellor,* 12: 235–41.

Rhodes, R., Hill, C.E., Thompson, B. and Elliott, R. (1994) 'A retrospective study of the client perception of misunderstanding of events', *Journal of Counseling Psychology,* 41: 473–83.

Rice, L.N. (1974) 'The evocative function of the therapist', in D.A. Wexler and L.N. Rice (eds), *Innovations in Client-Centered Therapy.* New York: Wiley. pp. 289–312.

Rice, L.N. and Saperia, E. (1984) 'Task analysis of the resolution of problematic reactions', in L.N. Rice and L.S. Greenberg (eds), *Patterns of Change: Intensive Analysis of Psychotherapy Process.* New York: Guilford. pp. 29–66.

Rogers, C.R. (1957) 'The necessary and sufficient conditions of therapeutic personality change', *Journal of Consulting Psychology,* 21: 95–103.

Rogers, C.R. (1959) 'A theory of therapy, personality and interpersonal relationships, as developed in the client-centered framework', in S. Koch (ed.), *Psychology: A Study of a Science, Volume 3. Formulations of the Person and the Social Contract.* New York: McGraw-Hill. pp. 184–256.

Rogers, C.R. (1961) *On Becoming a Person: A Therapist's View of Psychotherapy.* Boston: Houghton Mifflin.

Sachse, R. (1989) Contribution to D.J. Cain (ed.), 'Proposals for the future of client-centered and experiential psychotherapy', *Person-Centered Review,* 4: 11–26.

Safran, J.D, Muran, J.C. and Wallner Samstag, L. (1994) 'Resolving therapeutic alliance ruptures: A task analytic investigation', in A.O. Horvath and L.S. Greenberg (eds), *The Working Alliance: Theory, Research, and Practice*. New York: Wiley. pp. 225–55.

Sass, L.A. (1988) 'Humanism, hermeneutics, and the concept of the human subject', in S.B. Messer, L.A. Sass and R.L. Woolfolk (eds), *Hermeneutics and Psychological Theory*. New Brunswick: Rutgers University Press. pp. 222–71.

Searle, J. (1983) *Intentionality: An Essay in the Philosophy of Mind*. Cambridge: Cambridge University Press.

Seeman, J. (1988) 'Self-actualization: A reformulation', *Person-Centered Review*, 3: 304–15.

Shaul, A.N. (1994) ' "Therapists" symbolic visual imagery: A key to empathic understanding', *Dissertation Abstracts International*, 54: 5953-B. Order number: DANN84217.

Shlien, J.M. (1970) 'The literal-intuitive axis and other thoughts', in J.T. Hart and T.M. Tomlinson (eds), *New Directions in Client-Centered Therapy*. Boston: Houghton Mifflin. Cited in J.M. Shlien and R.F. Levant, 'Introduction', in R.F. Levant and J.M. Shlien (eds) (1984) *Client-Centered Therapy and the Person-Centered Approach: New Directions in Theory, Research and Practice*. New York: Praeger. pp. 1–16.

Shlien, J.M. (1996) 'Embarrassment anxiety: A literalist theory', in R. Hutterer, G. Pawlowsky, G. Schmid and R. Stipsits (eds), *Client-Centered and Experiential Psychotherapy: A Paradigm in Motion*. Frankfurt am Main and New York: Peter Lang. pp. 35–46.

Spence, D.P. (1982) *Narrative Truth and Historical Truth: Meaning and Interpretation in Psychoanalysis*. New York: Norton.

Sterba, R. (1934) 'The fate of the ego in analytic therapy', *International Journal of Psychoanalysis*, 15: 117–26.

Stolorow, R.D. and Atwood, G.E. (1992) *Contexts of Being: The Intersubjective Foundations of Psychological Life*. Hillsdale, NJ: The Analytic Press.

Sullivan, H.S. (1953) *The Interpersonal Theory of Psychiatry*. New York: Norton.

Taylor, C. (1985) *Philosophy and the Human Sciences: Philosophical Papers 2*. Cambridge: Cambridge University Press.

Taylor, C. (1989) *Sources of the Self: The Making of Modern Identity*. Cambridge, MA: Harvard University Press.

Thayer, H.S. (1968) *Meaning and Action: A Critical History of Pragmatism*. New York: Bobbs-Merrill.

Thorne, B. (1989) Contribution to D.J. Cain (ed.), 'Proposals for the future of client-centered and experiential psychotherapy', *Person-Centered Review*, 4: 11–26.

Toukmanian, S.G. (1986) 'A measure of client perceptual processing', in L.S. Greenberg and W.M. Pinsof (eds), *The Psychotherapeutic Process: A Research Handbook*. New York: Guilford. pp. 107–30.

Toukmanian, S.G. (1990) 'A schema-based information processing perspective on client change in experiential therapy', in G. Lietaer, J. Rombauts and R. Van Balen (eds), *Client-Centered and Experiential Therapy in the Nineties*. Leuven: Leuven University Press. pp. 309–26.

Toukmanian, S.G. (1992) 'Studying the client's perceptual processes and their outcomes', in S.G. Toukmanian and D.L. Rennie (eds), *Psychotherapy Process Research: Paradigmatic and Narrative Approaches*. Newbury Park, CA: Sage. pp. 77–107.

Toukmanian, S.G., Capelle, R.G. and Rennie, D.L. (1978) 'Counsellor trainee awareness of evaluative criteria: A neglected variable', *Canadian Counsellor*, 12: 177–83.

Toukmanian, S.G. and Rennie, D.L. (1975) 'Microcounseling versus human relations training: Relative effectiveness with undergraduate trainees', *Journal of Counseling Psychology*, 22: 345–53.

Truax, C.B. and Carkhuff, R.R. (1967) *Toward Effective Counseling and Psychotherapy: Training and Practice*. Chicago, IL: Aldine.

Van Belle, H.A. (1980) *Basic Intent and Therapeutic Approach of Carl Rogers: A Study of His View of Man in Relation to His View of Therapy, Personality and Interpersonal Relations*. Toronto: Wedge.

Watson, J.C. (1997) 'Manifesting clients' agency in experiential therapy', in A. Bohart (Chair), *The Client's Active Role in Change: Implications for Integration*, symposium presented at the annual meeting of the Society for the Exploration of Psychotherapy Integration, Toronto.

Watson, J.C. and Greenberg, L.S. (1994) 'The alliance in experiential therapy: Enacting the relationship conditions', in A.O. Horvath and L.S. Greenberg (eds), *The Working Alliance: Theory, Research and Practice*. New York: Wiley.

Watson, J.C. and Rennie, D.L. (1994) 'A qualitative analysis of clients' subjective experience of significant moments in therapy during the exploration of problematic reactions', *Journal of Counseling Psychology*, 41: 500–9.

Watson, N. (1984) 'The empirical status of Rogers's hypotheses of the necessary and sufficient conditions for effective psychotherapy', in R.F. Levant and J.M. Shlien (eds), *Client-Centered and the Person-Centered Approach: Directions in Theory, Research and Practice*. New York: Praeger.

Watzlawick, P., Beavin, J.H. and Jackson, D.D. (1967) *Pragmatics of Human Communication*. New York: Norton.

Wexler, D.A. (1974) 'A cognitive theory of experiencing self-actualization, and therapeutic process', in D.A. Wexler and L.N. Rice (eds), *Innovations in Client-Centered Therapy*. New York: Wiley. pp. 49–116.

Wood, J.K. (1996) 'The person-centered approach: Toward an understanding of its implications', in R. Hutterer, G. Pawlowsky, P.F. Schmid and R. Stipsits (eds), *Client-Centered and Experiential Psychotherapy: A Paradigm in Motion*. Frankfurt am Main: Peter Lang. pp. 163–84.

Zetzel, E.R. (1956) 'Current concepts of transference', *International Journal of Psychoanalysis*, 37: 369–76.

Zimring, F. (1990) 'A characteristic of Rogers's response to clients', *Person-Centered Review*, 5, 433–48.

Subject index

Acceptance, 63
  of client by counsellor, 14–15, 21, 30
  of counsellor by client, 16, 57, 63
Accuracy of responding, 38–40, 56, 58, 60, 118, 120–122
  client's, 37, 100
Actualization, 6
  criticisms of self-actualization, 7–8
  of organism, 6–7
  of self, 2, 6–8
Advice, 94–95, 98, 115
  impulse to give, 27, 34–36, 40
Agency, 3, 8, 11–12, 68, 91, 117, 122
  client's, 13–21, 24–25, 69, 79, 80–81, 89, 104
  counsellor's, 25
Ambiguity tolerance, 26–27
Assessment, 24, 34
  in person-centred counselling generally, 35
  need for, 35
Attention to client, 14–15, 24–26, 30, 33–34, 43, 60, 133

Basic attending skills, 32–43
Beginning counsellors, 127, 137, 140
  special anxieties, 22–23, 62, 66, 70
Bids for clarification, 36, 39–40
Body language, 14, 33–34, 74, 76, 89–90, 96, 120, 138

Change, 3, 8, 30, 68, 80, 107
  resistance to, 3, 7–8, 18, 23, 93
Co-construction of client's experience, 38, 51, 114
Cognitive privilege, 91, 104
  defined, 69
Cognitive therapy, iv, 90
Communication
  as purposes and impacts, 37, 90–92, 97, 99–100, 107, 118, 125
Compliance, 37, 97, 99, 102, 114–115
  willing, 115–117, 125
Confrontation, 65, 68, 74, 76, 99, 106, 112
Congruence, 7, 89, 91–92
  counsellor's, 9–10, 21, 30, 32–33, 43, 59–60, 70

Consciousness, iv, 3, 5, 13, 59, 89, 102, 114
Control, 25–26, 30, 41, 115
  client's, 1, 8, 19–20, 25, 30, 42, 113
  counsellor's, 1, 8, 118, 130
  in training, 131
Core conditions, 2, 6, 8–9, 21m, 32–33, 103
Counter-transference, 64, 91
  objective, 68
  subjective, 68–69, 101, 118
Covert experience, 5–6, 62, 75, 99–100, 104, 124
  client's, v, 17–18, 20, 28, 56–57, 110, 114, 119–122
Crisis in counselling, 26, 63–66, 70

Defensiveness, 3, 72
  client's, 65, 80, 108, 111–112
  counsellor's, 62
Deference, client's, 9, 15–18, 27, 50, 62, 70, 81, 92, 95–97, 99, 104, 107, 110, 124
Dewey's influence on Rogers, 4, 7, 10, 12
Disjunctions, 15, 57, 120
  counsellor's, 60, 62, 64–65, 143
  in the relationship, 17–19, 64–66, 99–101, 107, 114, 120
Dualism, 4, 10, 12, 90–91

Embodiment, 11, 87
  and feelings, 4
  and reflexivity, 2
Emotion, 5, 15, 35, 47, 49, 60, 72, 80–81, 114, 117
  schemes, 5–6, 11
Empathic responding, 2, 10, 49–50, 58, 112–113, 115, 120–122, 127, 132, 134, 140
  compared to process work, 73–80, 82–84, 92, 109–110, 117–118, 126, 138
Empathy, 7, 26, 30
  correlates of, 32, 34–35
Encounter, 64–66, 69
Ending the relationship, 107, 122–125, 130

Evaluation
  of client by counsellor, 18, 27, 36, 61, 64–66, 105, 113, 133
  of counsellor by client, 17, 20, 61–62, 64–65, 81, 94–97, 105, 120, 127
  difficulty in suspending, 61, 64
  importance of suspension of, 25–27, 30, 61
  trainee's self-, 132–133
Existential therapy, v, 7, 9, 11, 20, 44, 69, 91
Expectations about counselling
  client's, 22, 107, 109
  counsellor's, 16, 22–23, 33
Experiential therapy, iv–v, 2, 4, 9, 21, 32–33, 42, 82

Felt-sense, 4, 7, 11, 37, 42, 71–3, 75, 88, 104
  and essentialism, 4
  as direct referent, 4, 12, 37
  as exact form, 4, 12
  as leading edge, 9, 14
  as organismic valuing process, 7
  in training, 131, 133, 138
Feminist therapy, v, 19, 69, 91
First meeting, the, 22–31, 107
  closing, 109
Focusing, 5, 9, 12, 81

Gestalt therapy, 19, 75, 87

Hermeneutics, vi–vii, 12
Holism, 2, 11, 132
Homework, 19, 124
Hope, 24, 27
Humanism, iv–v, 10–11

Imagery, 44–51, 58–60, 118, 136
Incongruence, 7, 9, 92, 100
  client's, 20
  counsellor's, 60–64, 70
Information processing theory, 2, 11
Informed consent, 28–30, 113
Insight, 20, 86
Intentionality, 5, 42, 74–75, 103–104, 143
Internal reactions, counsellor's, 26, 43–45, 58, 61, 64–70, 76, 91, 117–118
  in training, 134, 137
Interpersonal Process Recall, 50, 53, 86–87, 90, 105–107, 120
Interpersonal therapy, v, 10–11, 44, 66, 69–70, 90, 100–101, 112, 136

Interpretation, 27, 34–35, 38, 40, 57, 77–79, 130–131
  client's experience as positive, 27, 35

Leading edge of client's experience, 2, 9, 42
  and felt-sense, 37, 43
  in training, 133–134
  working with, 51, 117–118
Limits to confidentiality, 28–30

Meaning, 48–49, 51–52, 58, 73–74, 76, 83, 88, 90
  quest for, 9, 36–37, 42, 44–45, 60, 88, 120
Metacommunication, vii, 1, 10, 45, 58–60, 69, 75, 83–84, 88–101
  and the working alliance, 91, 107–109, 118, 120–124
  compared to use in interpersonal therapy, 67, 90–91, 101
  four forms of, 97–101
  in training, 126, 132–138, 140
  Rogers's use of, 90, 118
Metaphor, 44–45, 51–58, 60, 90, 118
  and symbolic imagery, 48–51
Methodology of counselling research
  positivism, iv–v, 12
  qualitative approach, iv–v, 11
Microcounselling approach, 32
Minimal encouragements, 36, 40
Mistakes, 54, 57, 59, 62, 69, 122
  client's tolerance of, 16, 18, 39, 57, 59–60, 120–122
Modernism, 11–12

Narrative, 73–74, 108, 119–120
Non-reflexivity, 3–6, 11–12, 14, 20, 67, 87, 103–104, 143
  as an intention-in-action, 73, 143
Nonverbal behaviour/cues, 14, 32, 34, 62, 89–90, 103–104, 118, 120, 138

Object relations therapy, 66, 91
Ontology
  Gendlin's view of, 12
  Rogers's view of, vi, 4, 6
  supporting current approach, 103–104, 134

Paraphrases, 37–39, 118
Patient, on the client as, 8, 11, 13, 25, 68, 91, 100
Perceptual-processing therapy, 2, 5, 9, 11

Subject index

Person-centred counselling, iv, 42–44, 82, 113, 115, 140
 communication style, 30–34, 39–43
 literal, 1–2, 4–11, 21, 43, 69, 81, 90, 103, 108, 111, 120
 varieties of, vi, 1
Plans and strategies,
 client's, 17–18, 106
 conflicts about, 19, 94–97, 106, 114
 counsellor's, 54, 56
Positive regard,
 conditional, 6–7
 unconditional, 7
Postmodernism, iv, 10
Post-postmodernism, 11–12
Power
 imbalance, v, 44, 63, 70, 92, 100–101, 104, 114, 117, 120, 138
 struggles, 18–19
 therapeutic, 58–59
Problem solve
 impulse to, 23–25, 28, 34–36
Problematic reaction point, 5, 47
Process, 41–42, 121
 defined, 71
 direction, 1, 9, 12, 69, 81–83, 109, 119, 124
 learning how to do, 83–87, 132, 138–140, 141
 -experiential therapy, 2, 5–6, 10–11
 identification, 73–81, 119–120
 learning how to do, 83–87, 127, 132, 138–140
Psychoanalysis, vi, 64, 68, 90–91, 102–103, 112

Questions, 34, 108
 closed, 34–36, 39–40
 open-ended, 36, 40

Real relationship with counsellor, 68–69, 91–92, 100, 102, 104
Referential activity, 47–48
Reflection, 30, 38, 40, 54, 64, 79, 110, 118, 120
 evocative, 46–47, 118
Reflexivity, 2–6, 11–13, 68, 73, 89, 100, 103–104, 124, 132, 143
 defined, v, 1
 and disjunctions, 15
 client's, 1, 20–21

counsellor's, 63
 and the will, 115–116
Repetitions, 37
Resistance
 client's, 36, 51, 66, 76, 82, 90, 95, 113–114, 117, 121
 trainee's, 41, 83, 131, 134, 138
Roleplaying
 in counselling, 20, 96
 in training, 126–130, 138, 140, 142

Self, notion of, 3, 6, 10–12
Self-disclosure, 17, 44, 61–66, 70, 93
Self-focus, 13, 18, 22, 35, 42, 60, 92, 106, 114
Social constructionism, iv, 11
Support, 18, 63, 74, 93, 120–121
Symmetry
 in communication, 89, 91–92
 in the counselling relationship, 68

Technique, matter of, 10, 32–33, 67, 69, 82, 103
Tentativeness, 65, 79, 82, 140
Themes
 client's, 28, 51, 60, 123
 relationship, 18–19
 trainee's, 130–131
Track, client's, 13–15, 35, 42, 44–45, 47, 57–58, 75, 109, 120, 138
Training in use of current approach, 126–142
Transference, 67–68, 90–91, 102–104, 112
Transparency, 1, 43, 59–70, 89, 92, 132
 training in, 134–138

Unconscious, the, 3, 8, 48, 102, 104, 114

Verbal following behaviour, 36–40

Working alliance, 18–19, 25, 67–68, 81–82, 91–92, 101–125, 127
 development of, 104, 107–108, 125, 127
 maintenance of, 104, 107, 117–119, 125,
 repair of, 104, 107, 119–122, 125
 and Rogers, 102–103
 ruptures in, 105–106, 117, 119, 120–121
 training in developing, 130, 132–133, 137, 139–142

Author index

Alcorn, L., 34
Angel, R., 69
Angus, L.E., 48–49, 51–52, 90
Atwood, G.E., 103

Beavin, J.H., 90
Bohart, A., 17, 23
Bozarth, J.D., 4, 30, 43, 124
Brodley, B.T., 4, 12
Buber, M., 69, 103
Bucci, W., 47
Burke, H., 32, 34
Butler, J.M., 7

Capelle, R., 41
Carkhuff, R.R., 32

Descartes, R., 4, 10, 68, 90
Dewey, J., 4, 7, 10

Ellenberger, H.R., 91
Elliott, R., 2, 4–5, 9, 27, 50, 91

Ford, J.G., 7
Frankfurt, H., 116
Freud, S., 49, 102

Gendlin, E.T., 2, 4–6, 9–13, 16, 37, 50–51, 71
Greenberg, L.S., iv, 2, 4–7, 76, 102
Greenson, R., 67, 91, 102–103

Habermas, J., 12
Heidegger, M., 8
Hill, C.E., 105
Holdstock, L.T., 2
Horvath, A.O., 102
Husserl, E., 4

Ivey, A.E., 32, 36

James, W., 10, 14
Jackson, D.D., 90

Kagan, N., 50, 53
Kant, I., 10
Kiesler, D.J., 10, 52, 67–69, 90–91, 100

Laing, R.D., 91, 103
Leary, T.F., 67
Liejssen, M., 2, 4
Lietaer, G., 1–2, 9, 43
Locke, J., 6, 8, 90
Luborsky, L., 102

McLeod, J., iv, 91
Macmurray, J., 8
Maddi, S.R., 7–8
Margolis, J., 5, 12, 69
May, E., 41
May, R., 69

Mead, G.H., 10
Mearns, D., vi, 2, 6, 9, 43, 68
Merleau-Ponty, M., 4–5
Miller, L.A., 30
Muran, J.C., 9, 105, 114
Murphy, A.E., 7

Nichols, M., 41
Noble, S., 23

O'Hara, M.M., 2, 7, 103

Paivio, A., 47
Patterson, C.H., 4
Pearson, P.H., 13
Perls, F., 75
Phillips, J.R., 13

Quartaro, G.K., 41

Rennie, D.L., 1, 3–4, 6, 8, 13, 15–16, 19, 32, 34, 41–42, 49–52, 68–69, 74, 99, 105, 117, 119
Rhodes, R., 9, 105, 107
Rice, L.N., iv, 2, 5, 7, 44, 46–47, 118
Rogers, C.R., iv, 1, 4–12, 30, 32, 38, 43, 90, 102–103, 118, 143
Rousseau, J.J., 10

Sachse, R., 2
Safran, J.D., 9, 105, 114
Saperia, E., 2, 47
Sass, L.A., 4, 12
Searle, J., 3
Seeman, J. 8
Shaul, A.N., 50
Shlein, J.M., 1, 4, 30
Simek-Downing, L., 36
Spence, D.P., 103
Sullivan, H.S., 90

Tallman, K., 23
Taylor, C., 10, 116
Thayer, H.S., 7
Thorne, B., vi, 2, 9, 43, 68
Toukmanian, S.G., 2, 6, 11, 32, 34, 41, 119
Truax, C.B., 32

Van Belle, H.A., 4, 43, 69, 103

Wallner Samstag, 9, 105, 114
Watson, J.C., 6, 76
Watson, N., 35
Watzlawick, P., 90
Wexler, D.A., 4, 8, 13
Wood, J.K., 7

Zetzel, E.R., 67, 102
Zimring, F., 12